BATTLEBOTS

THE OFFICIAL GUIDE

BY MEL MAXWELL

SCHOLASTIC INC.

TABLE OF CONTENTS

FIGHT! FIGHT! FIGHT!

Welcome to the world of BattleBots! It's the hardest-hitting robot-splitting tournament of all time. Sparks fly, gears grind, metal crunches, flames sizzle—and that's all within the first few seconds of combat! When the spinning, shredding, and hammering escalates in the BattleBox, the ground quakes and the arena shakes. Crowds roar and bot builders sweat over their controllers as the clock counts down to total destruction, devastating carnage, and victory for those who reign supreme.

You've seen the action on your screens. Now get a bot's-eye view of the main event with this ultimate guidebook! Discover all the latest stats, facts, and pro tips on your favorite robots, from legendary veterans to outstanding rookies. You'll take an up-close look to see how they work, how they've evolved, and what gives them an edge in the competition. From traditional weaponry to the latest technology, these machines have been engineered with precision, grit, and creativity.

You will also meet the amazing teams behind these modern masterpieces. People from all over the globe and of all ages have risen to the challenge. Rocket scientists, Hollywood special-effects artists, hobby builders, and high school students have competed in the world's biggest and best robot fighting event. Anyone who dares to dream can rise to glory and win the coveted Giant Nut—even you!

So, what are you waiting for? It's robot fighting time!

GIGABYTE AND CAPTAIN SHREDERATOR

HIJINX AND SUBZERO

BLACKSMITH AND SHATTER!

SEEDS OF DESTRUCTION

For over two decades, bot builders have gathered to trade blows and wreak havoc in BattleBots tournaments. Legends have formed, the mighty have fallen, and new generations of rising stars continue to join the army of challengers. But where did it all begin? You might be surprised to learn that a battle of such epic proportions had very humble beginnings.

It all started in San Francisco in 1994 when cousins Trey Roski and Greg Munson got together with their friend Gage Cauchois. Their mission: Construct their very own robot fighter and enter it in Robot Wars, a local robot fighting contest founded by Marc Thorpe, the godfather of robot combat. Two months and six hundred dollars later, they built La Machine. Their creation went on to win trophies and even battled in Germany and England. By 1997, the team started an unofficial league to battle bots with neighbors and friends. As popularity grew for this underground robotics movement, larger events were organized.

In August 1999, the first BattleBots competition was held in Long Beach, California. The rest is history!

1999 LONG BEACH EVENT

BattleBots is a bona fide sport where metal-twisting, mind-blowing robots duke it out in a fight to the death. Like all other sports, you have to respect the rules of the competition to get the full experience.

When the green light flashes and the starting buzzer sounds, the match is under way. Each battle consists of a single three-minute bout. The goal is to completely destroy or disable your opponent. If you can't do that, a panel of judges declares a victory. They score each match based on three criteria: Damage, Aggression, and Control.

To compete in the BattleBots World Championship, all robot combat builders must construct a heavyweight bot or multiple bots, provided that the total weight is no more than 250 lbs (pounds). All bots take part in multiple qualifying fights. The aim is not just to win, but to win with style, for a Selection Committee watches every fight and selects the best 32 bots to take part in the BattleBots World Championships. From there, it's a knockout, winner-take-all tournament. In the end, only one will take the title of World Champion and win the Giant Nut!

THE GIANT NUT

ANNOUNCERS CHRIS ROSE AND KENNY FLORIAN

HUGE AND SWITCHBACK

FARUQ TAUHEED GETS
THE CROWD EXCITED

Take an arena-side tour of the place where all the action happens: the BattleBox! This incredible feat of engineering is built for maximum safety on the outside, maximum torture on the inside, and maximum entertainment for spectators. Over the years, the BattleBox has been updated many times to heighten the conflict and raise the stakes. Check out the latest designs and mind-blowing stats of this fierce battleground.

The BattleBox is a fully enclosed, 35-ton arena made of steel and bulletproof "glass." It is raised two feet off the ground, and the walls and ceiling are not actually glass but an especially strong, transparent, reinforced, and multilayered polycarbonate, like the type used for aircraft windows. This special material is an inch and a quarter thick, and the walls are 24 feet high, with an enclosed roof to contain shrapnel and flying bot parts. The floor measures 48 x 48 feet and contains a red and blue square at each side. These squares are the starting positions for the competitors.

The teams get the best seats in the house. Their driving platforms offer an unflinching view of the arena, allowing them to strategize, talk smack, and navigate their robots through the perils of the BattleBox.

OUTSIDE THE BOX

INSIDE THE BOX

The BattleBox is a minefield of hazards. Sharp spikes, serrated screws, and pulverizing hammers controlled by the teams can annihilate even the toughest robots. And what lurks beneath? In the last minute of fighting, the KillSaws emerge from the floor! Take a look at all the torture devices that lie within the box.

SPIKE STRIP

The perimeter of the BattleBox is studded with a double-layered array of steel spikes designed to keep bots off the walls and inside the Box.

PULVERIZERS

These heavy-duty aluminum sledgehammers pack a mighty wallop in the corners of the arena. Avoid these at all costs, otherwise you could be pulverized into oblivion! Each team controls two of the four pulverizers and can try to maneuver the opposition underneath them.

THE SCREWS

Huge corkscrews churn and grind along the edges of the BattleBox. These bad boys can deliver bot-crunching punishment. They are reversible—once a bot gets stuck, the screws can change direction and spit it back out.

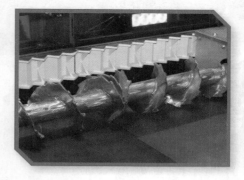

KILLSAWS

Titanium KillSaw blades are powered by a 220-volt, 3.5-horsepower motor, which can easily lift and damage a 250-lb robot. The sparks within the KillSaw mechanism fly 20 feet into the air at the start of each Main Event.

UPPER DECK

A 16-foot x 8-foot raised platform creates deadly short corners. Launching an opponent to the upper deck creates more opportunities for contact and knockouts.

These torture devices are auto-mated by the WOPR—the Weapons Operation Programmable Remote. This impressive control panel looks like it's from a sci-fi movie!

BEST OF THE BOTS

Are you ready to meet some of the most iconic bots and builders of all time? Come face-to-face with the brains, brawn, and brilliance behind the competition. This is your backstage pass to get a look at all the pushers, grabbers, flippers, spinners, slashers, hammers, wedges, lifters, crushers, and launchers. See how elite teams use state-of-the-art hardware to equip their bots with blades, hammers, axes, air cannons, clamps, jaws, discs, drums, catapults, plows, and even flamethrowers! From the weird and wacky to the sleek and supreme, you've never seen anything like this.

As you go through this hall of fame, you can rate each bot and note down your favorite features. Real builders and teams are always scoping out the competition to develop their fighting strategies and customize their killing machines. BattleBots isn't just a battle of physical strength—it's a war of wits and know-how.

HFA, THE TEAM BEHIND BLACKSMITH

FREE SHIPPING AND TOMBSTONE

PREPPING FOR BATTLE IN THE PIT

BACKSTAGE IN THE PIT

This farm-fresh bot is the cream of the crop! Its name comes from the bale spears that are used in farming to raise hay bales onto truck beds. The steel poker is designed to attack from above when this box-shaped robot climbs on top of its opponent.

HOMETOWN: SALEM, NEW JERSEY

TYPE: POKER

TOTAL MATCHES: 9

WIN PERCENTAGE: 11%

WINS: 1

LOSSES: 8

KNOCKOUTS: 1

KO PERCENTAGE: 11%

AVERAGE KNOCKOUT TIME: 58 SECONDS

Farm silo shields the poker

Chunky wheels with grip for maneuverability

Bale Spear

Bale Spear

Pneumatic poker made from 4130 steel

MEET THE TEAM

Forge and Farm Combat Robots are a three-man team led by captain Earl B. Pancoast III. As well as a robot builder and tinkerer, Earl is a real-life farmer. Bale Spear has even been adapted with GPS to patrol Earl's farm and scare away deer!

FULL TEAM

Earl B. Pancoast III, Malcolm Matheson, Miro Matheson

RATE THIS BOT!

☐	☐	☐	☐	☐
1	2	3	4	5
NOT MY TYPE	KINDA COOL	A SOLID BOT	SO AWESOME!	BEST OF THE BEST

FAVORITE FEATURES:

BEST ADVANTAGE IN BATTLE:

It's hammer time! Beta is a four-wheel-driven robot with a heavy-hitting, nitrogen-powered hammer. The crushing blows from its giant weapon can completely disable an opponent. Beta is a complex machine that deploys its hammer strategically, while also relying on its mobility and defensive design.

HOMETOWN: OXFORD, UNITED KINGDOM

TYPE: HAMMER

TOTAL MATCHES: 9

WIN PERCENTAGE: 67%

WINS: 6

LOSSES: 3

KNOCKOUTS: 3

KO PERCENTAGE: 33%

AVERAGE KNOCKOUT TIME: 147 SECONDS

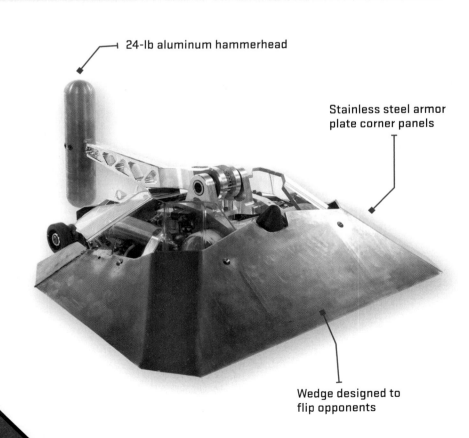

24-lb aluminum hammerhead

Stainless steel armor plate corner panels

Wedge designed to flip opponents

MEET THE TEAM

Team Hurtz is run by team captain John Reid, a design engineer. He comes all the way from the United Kingdom. John is known as one of the best drivers in the competition, who skillfully drives Beta around the BattleBox.

FULL TEAM

Alan Cannon, Gabriel Stroud, John Reid

RATE THIS BOT!

☐	☐	☐	☐	☐
1	**2**	**3**	**4**	**5**
NOT MY TYPE	KINDA COOL	A SOLID BOT	SO AWESOME!	BEST OF THE BEST

FAVORITE FEATURES:

BEST ADVANTAGE IN BATTLE:

BITE FORCE

Bite Force has won the Giant Nut three times, making it one of the most legendary fighters of all time. Its name comes from "bite force quotient" (BFQ), which measures the crushing force in an animal's jaw. The knockout power of Bite Force's vertical spinning bar dishes out pain and punishment to annihilate the competition.

HOMETOWN: MOUNTAIN VIEW, CALIFORNIA

TYPE: BAR SPINNER (VERTICAL)

TOTAL MATCHES: 27

WIN PERCENTAGE: 96%

WINS: 26

LOSSES: 1

KNOCKOUTS: 17

KO PERCENTAGE: 68%

AVERAGE KNOCKOUT TIME: 81 SECONDS

Asymmetrical vertical spinning bar

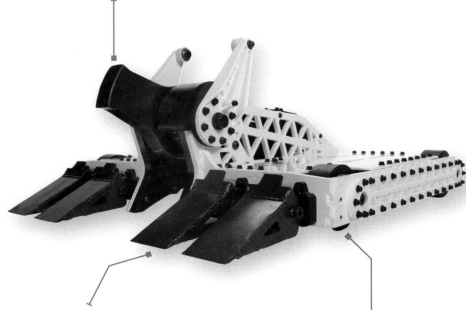

Blue forks mounted to the front for defense

Runs on four wheels, but was originally built on tracks

MEET THE TEAM

Paul Ventimiglia is the captain of APTYX Designs, a competitive team of engineers and friends in Silicon Valley, California. He was still a college student at Worcester Polytechnic Institute when he won $500,000 from NASA for building a robot called Moonraker to dig moon dirt. Paul is married to fellow teammate Teena Liu—they kiss before every fight!

FULL TEAM

Cory McBride, Jeremiah Jinno, Paul Ventimiglia, Rob Masek, Teena Liu, Tim Bogdanof, Travis Covington

RATE THIS BOT!

☐	☐	☐	☐	☐
1	**2**	**3**	**4**	**5**
NOT MY TYPE	KINDA COOL	A SOLID BOT	SO AWESOME!	BEST OF THE BEST

FAVORITE FEATURES:

BEST ADVANTAGE IN BATTLE:

Eggbeaters aren't just for the kitchen—the primary weapon on this major bot from Brazil is a 50-lb egg beater spinner! This box-shaped basher is tough and durable. It has won battles even while engulfed in flames. Its weapon isn't just for attacking, either. If Black Dragon gets flipped over, the spinner can be deployed at full speed to flip it back over.

HOMETOWN: ITAJUBÁ, BRAZIL

TYPE: EGG BEATER SPINNER

TOTAL MATCHES: 21

WIN PERCENTAGE: 71%

WINS: 15

LOSSES: 6

KNOCKOUTS: 8

KO PERCENTAGE: 38%

AVERAGE KNOCKOUT TIME: 84 SECONDS

Runs on two wheels

Egg beater spinner has teeth cut into it

Front wedge can throw opponents into the air

MEET THE TEAM

Team Uai!rrior is an elite Brazilian crew that formed in 2001 at the Federal University of Itajubá (UNIFEI). Over the years, they have built more than a dozen combat bots and won the BattleBots Desperado Tournament in 2019. Their team mascot is a duck called Mano!

FULL TEAM

Felipe Duarte, Gabriel Gomes, João Marcos, Mateus Cintra, Moises Araujo, Nicholas Santana, Tarcisio Rezende, Vinicius Malaquias

RATE THIS BOT!

☐	☐	☐	☐	☐
1	**2**	**3**	**4**	**5**
NOT MY TYPE	KINDA COOL	A SOLID BOT	SO AWESOME!	BEST OF THE BEST

FAVORITE FEATURES:

BEST ADVANTAGE IN BATTLE:

BLACKSMITH

Blacksmith brings the heat and burns up the BattleBox. Its power hammer doesn't just slam down on opponents—it shoots fire! The asymmetrical green disc is linked to a gear chain and weapon shaft. The steel armor on this bulky, square bot is configured to withstand gashes from vertical spinners.

HOMETOWN: EDISON, NEW JERSEY

TYPE: POWER HAMMER

TOTAL MATCHES: 19

WIN PERCENTAGE: 42%

WINS: 8

LOSSES: 11

KNOCKOUTS: 3

KO PERCENTAGE: 16%

AVERAGE KNOCKOUT TIME: 166 SECONDS

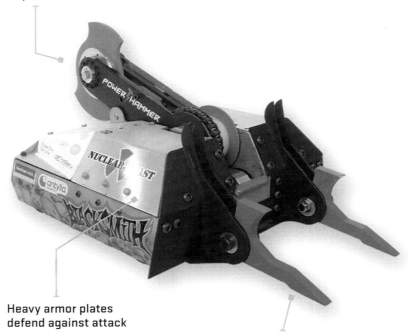

Flamethrower mounted to the power hammer

Heavy armor plates defend against attack

Long forks ram into opponents

MEET THE TEAM

Team HFA is led by electromechanical technician Al Kindle, a seasoned veteran of robotic combat. Al's first-ever match was against BattleBots founders Trey Roski and Greg Munson in 1995. HFA stands for Half Fast Astronaut.

FULL TEAM

Al Kindle, Alan Young, Earl B. Pancoast III, James Iocca, John Wolan, Kyle Singer

RATE THIS BOT!				
☐	☐	☐	☐	☐
1	**2**	**3**	**4**	**5**
NOT MY TYPE	KINDA COOL	A SOLID BOT	SO AWESOME!	BEST OF THE BEST

FAVORITE FEATURES:

BEST ADVANTAGE IN BATTLE:

BLIP

This high-energy four-wheel bot is the most compact flipper in the competition. Its primary weapon is a powerful rear-hinged kinetic flipper that uses flywheel energy storage. Blip's long forks at the front are designed to help the flipper get underneath opponents. Don't let its cute eyes fool you—Blip is here to cause major damage!

HOMETOWN: MOUNTAIN VIEW, CALIFORNIA

TYPE: LAUNCHER

TOTAL MATCHES: 7

WIN PERCENTAGE: 86%

WINS: 6

LOSSES: 1

KNOCKOUTS: 5

KO PERCENTAGE: 71%

AVERAGE KNOCKOUT TIME: 107 SECONDS

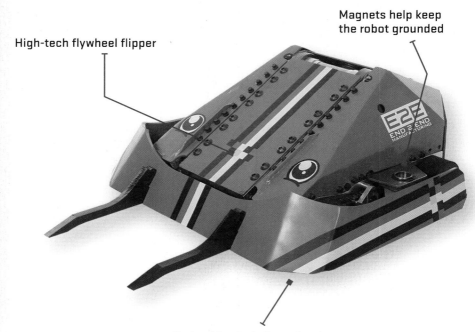

High-tech flywheel flipper

Magnets help keep the robot grounded

Underside made from titanium

MEET THE TEAM

Seems Reasonable Robotics is a team of engineers and builders. Their expertise isn't just limited to robotic combat. Team captain Aren Hill won a Power Wheels Racing Series in a snail-themed electric go-kart built by Seems Reasonable! Seems Reasonable Robotics also built Tantrum, which won the Giant Nut in 2021.

FULL TEAM

Alec Kochis, Alex Grant, Aren Hill, Brian Silverman, Bryan Culver, David Mintz, Dillon Carey, Erica Chin, Ginger Schmidt, James Doherty, Jason Weihman, Katie Widen, Kristine Atiyeh, Max Chang, Sean Doherty, Steven Silverman, Sue Doherty, Will Stanley, Zach Marks

RATE THIS BOT!

☐	☐	☐	☐	☐
1	2	3	4	5
NOT MY TYPE	KINDA COOL	A SOLID BOT	SO AWESOME!	BEST OF THE BEST

FAVORITE FEATURES:

BEST ADVANTAGE IN BATTLE:

BLOODSPORT

This blood-splattered bot is totally packed with weaponry. Bloodsport has four different steel weapon bars that range from 57 to 77 lbs. There is a long bar, a disc, a tribar, and a key blade. Its primary weapon is powered by four motors that allow it to reach a top speed of 250 mph (miles per hour).

HOMETOWN: CAMBRIDGE, MASSACHUSETTS

TYPE: BAR SPINNER (HORIZONTAL)

TOTAL MATCHES: 24

WIN PERCENTAGE: 63%

WINS: 15

LOSSES: 9

KNOCKOUTS: 10

KO PERCENTAGE: 42%

AVERAGE KNOCKOUT TIME: 84 SECONDS

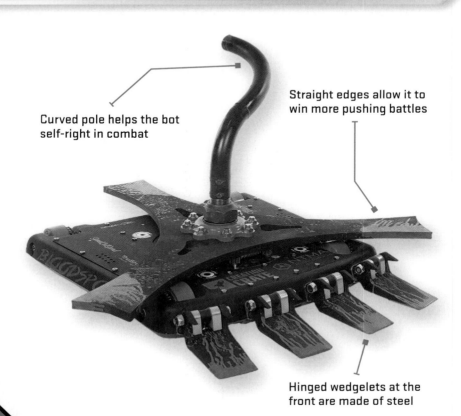

Curved pole helps the bot self-right in combat

Straight edges allow it to win more pushing battles

Hinged wedgelets at the front are made of steel

MEET THE TEAM

Bots 'n' Stuff Robotics formed in 2014. Before every battle, the team performs a special ritual: They dance around Bloodsport while attaching the weapon blade. Their team captain, Justin Marple, is a dynamo behind the controller.

FULL TEAM

Aaron Lucas, Andrew Marple, Claus Buchholz, Jordan Kiesel, Justin Marple, Katie Mumford, Matt Marple, Nik Buchholz, Owen Marshall, Rosa Ruiz, Seth Schaffer

RATE THIS BOT!

☐	☐	☐	☐	☐
1	**2**	**3**	**4**	**5**
NOT MY TYPE	KINDA COOL	A SOLID BOT	SO AWESOME!	BEST OF THE BEST

FAVORITE FEATURES:

BEST ADVANTAGE IN BATTLE:

Get ready to flip out! Over the years that Bronco competed, it wowed audiences with its showstopping weapon: a powerful pneumatic arm that effortlessly flipped opponents and threw them around the BattleBox. Its interchangeable armor pieces allowed this bot to adapt to different contenders in multiple tournaments.

HOMETOWN: SAUSALITO, CALIFORNIA

TYPE: LAUNCHER

TOTAL MATCHES: 19

WIN PERCENTAGE: 58%

WINS: 11

LOSSES: 8

KNOCKOUTS: 9

KO PERCENTAGE: 47%

AVERAGE KNOCKOUT TIME: 66 SECONDS

Tail armor can fend off opponents

Top armor designed to deal with hammers

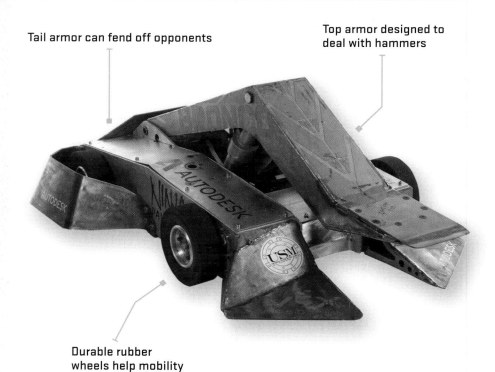

Durable rubber wheels help mobility

MEET THE TEAM

Alexander "Zander" Rose and Reason Bradley were childhood friends who went on to form Inertia Labs, the team behind Bronco. Outside of BattleBots, Alexander shares several design patents on the Clock of the Long Now, a mechanical clock that is designed to keep time for 10,000 years.

FULL TEAM

Alexander "Zander" Rose, Nolan Van Dine, Reason Bradley, Scoutt Balchowsky

RATE THIS BOT!

☐ 1	☐ 2	☐ 3	☐ 4	☐ 5
NOT MY TYPE	KINDA COOL	A SOLID BOT	SO AWESOME!	BEST OF THE BEST

FAVORITE FEATURES:

BEST ADVANTAGE IN BATTLE:

CAPTAIN SHREDERATOR

Captain Shrederator is one of the longest-competing fighters in BattleBots history. The spinning shell on this stone-cold killer can tear pieces out of anything that gets in its way. Depending on its opponent, it uses different sizes and shapes of weapon teeth to get the best possible bite.

HOMETOWN: ORMOND BEACH, FLORIDA

TYPE: FULL-BODIED SPINNER

TOTAL MATCHES: 21

WIN PERCENTAGE: 29%

WINS: 6

LOSSES: 15

KNOCKOUTS: 6

KO PERCENTAGE: 29%

AVERAGE KNOCKOUT TIME: 107 SECONDS

Spinning shell doubles
as a shield of armor

360-degree range of attack

Each end of the bot
has a dedicated motor

MEET THE TEAM

Team LOGICOM is one of the most successful teams in BattleBots, with over 20 years in competition. They won a Giant Nut in 2002 with a different robot, Phrizbee Ultimate. Captain Shrederator was built by Brian Nave, a retired electrical engineer who is also the team captain.

FULL TEAM

Brian Hauch, Brian Nave, Christopher Nave, Geno Esposito, Jonathan La Plain, Ken Bryant, Nick Nave

RATE THIS BOT!

☐	☐	☐	☐	☐
1	**2**	**3**	**4**	**5**
NOT MY TYPE	KINDA COOL	A SOLID BOT	SO AWESOME!	BEST OF THE BEST

FAVORITE FEATURES:

BEST ADVANTAGE IN BATTLE:

Most bots roll . . . Chomp walks on legs! It has six gas-powered legs and feet it uses to crab around the arena. It uses compressed gas to power both its 18 leg joints and its mega hammer! The word for using compressed gas like this is "pneumatic." Because of its unique ability to walk, Chomp has a special dispensation to allow it to be heavier than the usual 250 lbs.

HOMETOWN: BURBANK, CALIFORNIA

TYPE: WALKER & HAMMER

TOTAL MATCHES: 16

WIN PERCENTAGE: 31%

WINS: 5

LOSSES: 11

KNOCKOUTS: 2

KO PERCENTAGE: 13%

AVERAGE KNOCKOUT TIME: 116 SECONDS

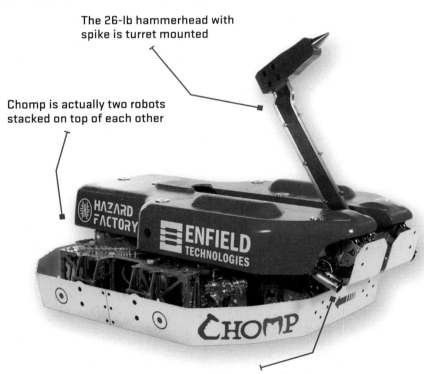

The 26-lb hammerhead with spike is turret mounted

Chomp is actually two robots stacked on top of each other

Flamethrowers unleash fire on opponents

MEET THE TEAM

The Machine Corps is led by mechanical engineer Zoe Stephenson, and has won a BattleBots Founder's Award and the Grant Imahara Award for Best Design. During the building of Chomp, the team had up to six different people simultaneously programming and machining parts. Read more about Chomp on page 123.

FULL TEAM

Anonymous 1, Anonymous 2, Carina Wine, Dimitar Vassilev, Ellen Lackermann, Evan Finkle, Jascha Little, Matt Scott, Neal Chapman, Rachel Mark, Randy Maniccia, Rusty Oliver, Zoe Stephenson

RATE THIS BOT!

☐	☐	☐	☐	☐
1	**2**	**3**	**4**	**5**
NOT MY TYPE	KINDA COOL	A SOLID BOT	SO AWESOME!	BEST OF THE BEST

FAVORITE FEATURES:

BEST ADVANTAGE IN BATTLE:

CLAW VIPER

This fast-moving fighter has a need for speed! Claw Viper rushes around the arena faster than any bot in the competition. Its top speed comes from four RV-100E brushless motors paired to each wheel. These motors are usually used to power heavy spinning weaponry, but Claw Viper runs on them for acceleration.

HOMETOWN: SEATTLE, WASHINGTON

TYPE: GRAPPLER

TOTAL MATCHES: 9

WIN PERCENTAGE: 33%

WINS: 3

LOSSES: 6

KNOCKOUTS: 2

KO PERCENTAGE: 22%

AVERAGE KNOCKOUT TIME: 116 SECONDS

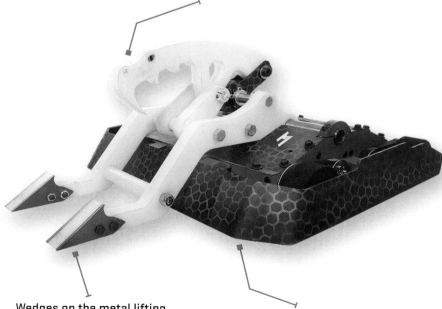

Plastic snake head clamps down to take a vicious bite

Wedges on the metal lifting forks can pick up opponents

Sloped armor at the front and sides doubles as wheel protection

MEET THE TEAM

Team Bad Ideas is led by software engineer Kevin Milczewski, who has had previous experience driving combat robots. Despite the team's name, they have plenty of *good* ideas to ensure Claw Viper keeps building its profile as an exciting newcomer.

FULL TEAM

Brian Adamson, Dan Bostian, Kevin Milczewski, Mike Thompson

RATE THIS BOT!

☐	☐	☐	☐	☐
1	**2**	**3**	**4**	**5**
NOT MY TYPE	KINDA COOL	A SOLID BOT	SO AWESOME!	BEST OF THE BEST

FAVORITE FEATURES:

BEST ADVANTAGE IN BATTLE:

Originally built in the United Kingdom, this British bot is a global force of domination! Cobalt's wedge-shaped body flips over opponents, and its vertical flywheel has sharp teeth that can slash tough steel. It's no wonder this fierce machine has previously won the Most Destructive Robot award.

HOMETOWN: OCEANSIDE, CALIFORNIA

TYPE: DISC SPINNER (VERTICAL)

TOTAL MATCHES: 13

WIN PERCENTAGE: 54%

WINS: 7

LOSSES: 6

KNOCKOUTS: 6

KO PERCENTAGE: 46%

AVERAGE KNOCKOUT TIME: 82 SECONDS

Asymmetrical vertical spinner is a weapon of mass destruction

Front wedge can get underneath opponents

Four wheels protected by steep armor

MEET THE TEAM

The Robotic Death Company has competed for many years with other heavyweight robots. This California-based crew took over the ownership of Cobalt from its original UK builders. That means Cobalt is the first BattleBots competitor to have been entered by both a UK and a US team!

FULL TEAM

Blair Lindberg, Brent Rieker, Camden Wallraff, Carol Williams, John Mladenik, Liz Mladenik, Matt Maxham, Melissa Mladenik, Micha Chewy Lebowitz, Mike Lindberg, Wendy Maxham

RATE THIS BOT!

☐	☐	☐	☐	☐
1	**2**	**3**	**4**	**5**
NOT MY TYPE	KINDA COOL	A SOLID BOT	SO AWESOME!	BEST OF THE BEST

FAVORITE FEATURES:

BEST ADVANTAGE IN BATTLE:

COPPERHEAD

Persistence is key for this fan favorite, as Copperhead maintains a steady streak of top performances. This two-wheel-drive invertible robot has an S7 tool steel, single-toothed, spinning drum. Copperhead is one of the smallest robots in the competition, but it packs one heck of a punch.

HOMETOWN: ERIE, COLORADO

TYPE: DRUM SPINNER

TOTAL MATCHES: 16

WIN PERCENTAGE: 63%

WINS: 10

LOSSES: 6

KNOCKOUTS: 6

KO PERCENTAGE: 38%

AVERAGE KNOCKOUT TIME: 76 SECONDS

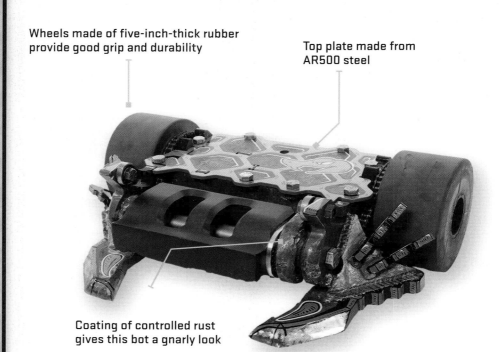

Wheels made of five-inch-thick rubber provide good grip and durability

Top plate made from AR500 steel

Coating of controlled rust gives this bot a gnarly look

MEET THE TEAM

Team Caustic Creations is the first team to have brought a live snake to a BattleBots competition! Their team mascot is Cuddles, an albino red tail boa. Although they are based in Colorado, original team captain Zach Goff is originally from Texas, where real copperhead snakes can be found.

FULL TEAM

Brad Henkel, Chad New, Cuddles, Kimberly Cowan, Luke Quintal, Micah Spinelli, Robert Cowan, Zach Goff

RATE THIS BOT!

☐	☐	☐	☐	☐
1	**2**	**3**	**4**	**5**
NOT MY TYPE	KINDA COOL	A SOLID BOT	SO AWESOME!	BEST OF THE BEST

FAVORITE FEATURES:

BEST ADVANTAGE IN BATTLE:

DOUBLE JEOPARDY

Ready, aim, fire! The air cannon on this robot can fire up to three shots in a single round of battle. It also has an onboard camera that helps it aim during fights. With its six wheels and sleek design, Double Jeopardy has supreme maneuverability around the arena.

HOMETOWN: IRVINE, CALIFORNIA

TYPE: SHOOTER

TOTAL MATCHES: 6

WIN PERCENTAGE: 14%

WINS: 1

LOSSES: 5

KNOCKOUTS: 1

KO PERCENTAGE: 17%

AVERAGE KNOCKOUT TIME: 158 SECONDS

Drive system has six brushless motors to power six internal wheels

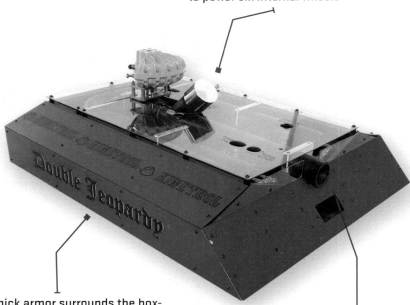

Thick armor surrounds the box-shaped robot for protection

Cannon fires metal slugs that can reach 250 mph for devastating impact

MEET THE TEAM

Team Double Trouble was founded by Evan and Bryce Woolley, twin brothers who are both lawyers by trade. These guys mean business—literally. They wear formal business suits and ties at every fight! Their robot is even named after a legal term called "double jeopardy."

FULL TEAM

Bill Woolley, Bryce Woolley, Evan Woolley

RATE THIS BOT!

☐	☐	☐	☐	☐
1	**2**	**3**	**4**	**5**
NOT MY TYPE	KINDA COOL	A SOLID BOT	SO AWESOME!	BEST OF THE BEST

FAVORITE FEATURES:

BEST ADVANTAGE IN BATTLE:

Duck for cover when this bot bird enters the arena. The "beak" lifter opens and closes like a duck's bill for snapping and lifting. It even makes quacking sounds from a built-in speaker! But don't let its cuteness trick you. DUCK! is a defensive demon that is built for endurance. It's one of the most durable robots in the competition.

HOMETOWN: PALO ALTO, CALIFORNIA

TYPE: LIFTER

TOTAL MATCHES: 14

WIN PERCENTAGE: 29%

WINS: 4

LOSSES: 10

KNOCKOUTS: 3

KO PERCENTAGE: 21%

AVERAGE KNOCKOUT TIME: 119 SECONDS

Built low to the ground to help get underneath opponents

Entire chassis made from magnesium, which is light but very strong

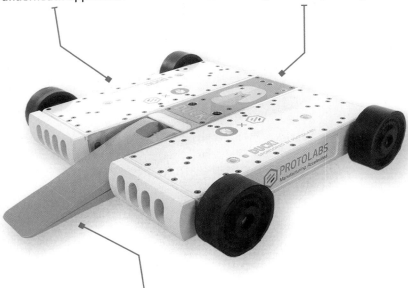

Thick steel plow provides defense against horizontal spinners

MEET THE TEAM

Team Black and Blue includes a family of robot enthusiasts. Inventor Hal Rucker, who has 20 years of experience in robotics, leads the team alongside his wife, Kathy. Their daughter, Hannah, is a vital team member who has operated DUCK!'s lifter while Hal drives the robot.

FULL TEAM

Dave Lyons, Hannah Rucker, Hal Rucker, Julia Chernuschevich, Kathy Rucker, Piper Lyons

RATE THIS BOT!

☐	☐	☐	☐	☐
1	**2**	**3**	**4**	**5**
NOT MY TYPE	KINDA COOL	A SOLID BOT	SO AWESOME!	BEST OF THE BEST

FAVORITE FEATURES:

BEST ADVANTAGE IN BATTLE:

Coming all the way from New Zealand, End Game is a world-class fighter and the first international winner of the Giant Nut. It became BattleBots' World Champion in 2020. The secret to its success is the powerful vertical spinner, which can reach upward of 6,000 rpm (revolutions per minute) in just five seconds. That's a LOT of slashing!

HOMETOWN: AUCKLAND, NEW ZEALAND

TYPE: DISC SPINNER (VERTICAL)

TOTAL MATCHES: 27

WIN PERCENTAGE: 70%

WINS: 19

LOSSES: 8

KNOCKOUTS: 17

KO PERCENTAGE: 63%

AVERAGE KNOCKOUT TIME: 90 SECONDS

50-lb spinning disc can tear through two inches of steel

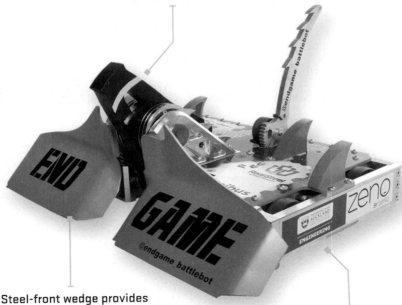

Steel-front wedge provides defense in the arena

Frame built out of aluminum to withstand destruction

MEET THE TEAM

The OYES Robotics team is led by Nick Mabey, a mechatronics engineer and graduate of the Auckland University Faculty of Engineering. The team is made up of seven members across New Zealand and the United States. This global group works thousands of hours a year to build and compete in BattleBots.

FULL TEAM

Christina Yu, Emma McMillan, Hammond Pearce, Jack Barker, Nick Mabey, Shane de Rijk, Steven Barker

RATE THIS BOT!

☐	☐	☐	☐	☐
1	**2**	**3**	**4**	**5**
NOT MY TYPE	KINDA COOL	A SOLID BOT	SO AWESOME!	BEST OF THE BEST

FAVORITE FEATURES:

BEST ADVANTAGE IN BATTLE:

Free Shipping pushes, slams, and outmaneuvers its opponents all around the BattleBox. This four-wheeled, boxlike robot always puts on a sizzling show, making it a fan favorite. Its forklift design features an array of cool weaponry: a lifting arm with sharp forks and the biggest flamethrower in the competition.

HOMETOWN: SAN LEANDRO, CALIFORNIA

TYPE: LIFTER

TOTAL MATCHES: 15

WIN PERCENTAGE: 33%

WINS: 5

LOSSES: 10

KNOCKOUTS: 2

KO PERCENTAGE: 13%

AVERAGE KNOCKOUT TIME: 73 SECONDS

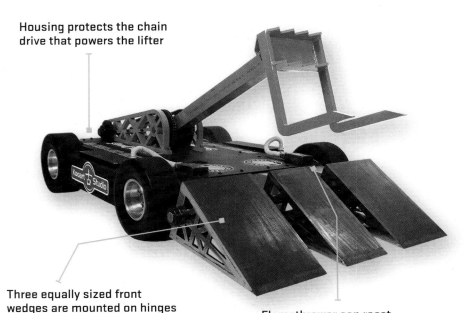

Housing protects the chain drive that powers the lifter

Three equally sized front wedges are mounted on hinges

Flamethrower can roast opponents in the BattleBox

MEET THE TEAM

Free Shipping was built by Gary Gin, the captain of Team Special Delivery. Gary is one of the most respected builders and drivers of all time. His finesse and control in driving has earned him multiple awards over years of robotic combat competition.

FULL TEAM

Eric Gin, Forrest Yeh, Gary Gin, Jim Yeh, Michael Strange, Roland Saekow

RATE THIS BOT!

☐	☐	☐	☐	☐
1	**2**	**3**	**4**	**5**
NOT MY TYPE	KINDA COOL	A SOLID BOT	SO AWESOME!	BEST OF THE BEST

FAVORITE FEATURES:

BEST ADVANTAGE IN BATTLE:

This pentagonal killing machine is packed with powerful weapons: not one but two spinners! A triangular disc at the front spins vertically for maximum aggression, while a rear horizontal disc reaches 250 mph. Fusion has two wheels on the top and two wheels underneath. That means it can keep rolling if it's inverted upside down!

HOMETOWN: DORCHESTER, WISCONSIN

TYPE: BI-WEAPON VERTICAL/HORIZONTAL COMBO

TOTAL MATCHES: 9

WIN PERCENTAGE: 44%

WINS: 4

LOSSES: 5

KNOCKOUTS: 4

KO PERCENTAGE: 44%

AVERAGE KNOCKOUT TIME: 58 SECONDS

Dual weaponry can spin when Fusion is upside down

AR500 steel armor provides strong protection

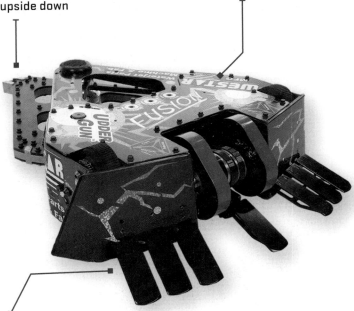

Ground-scraping wedgelets on either side

MEET THE TEAM

Team Whyachi Robotics is mostly made up of the Ewert family from Wisconsin. Reese Ewert is the builder and driver of Fusion. He's been building robots since he was a kid! The team has a tradition of eating Taco Bell every night of the competition.

FULL TEAM

Elizabeth Ewert, Luke Ewert, Pedro Vela, Rachel Trantow, Reese Ewert, Richard Stuplich, Terry Ewert, Trevor Trantrow

RATE THIS BOT!

☐	☐	☐	☐	☐
1	**2**	**3**	**4**	**5**
NOT MY TYPE	KINDA COOL	A SOLID BOT	SO AWESOME!	BEST OF THE BEST

FAVORITE FEATURES:

BEST ADVANTAGE IN BATTLE:

GHOST RAPTOR

Ghost Raptor has been competing for nearly a decade and has the scars to prove it. This robot has been snapped, crushed, and pulverized, but always lives to fight another day . . . just like a ghost! Although Ghost Raptor's design has been tweaked over the years, it has always featured a powerful bar spinner as its main weapon.

HOMETOWN: SAN JOSE, CALIFORNIA

TYPE: BAR SPINNER (HORIZONTAL)

TOTAL MATCHES: 16

WIN PERCENTAGE: 38%

WINS: 6

LOSSES: 10

KNOCKOUTS: 3

KO PERCENTAGE: 19%

AVERAGE KNOCKOUT TIME: 54 SECONDS

Forks can be deployed as a lifting weapon

Four-wheel drive for solid maneuverability

Flamethrower functions as a fiery secondary weapon

MEET THE TEAM

Team Raptor has been building and battling bots for over twenty years, and their experience shows! Lifters, spinners, crushers, even a giant axe—this team has built it all. If there's a competition to be had, you can expect Team Raptor to be there, carving their way through the ranks!

FULL TEAM

Chuck Pitzer, Anouk Wipprecht, Eric Diehr, Sabri Sansoy, Xo Wang

RATE THIS BOT!				
☐	☐	☐	☐	☐
1	**2**	**3**	**4**	**5**
NOT MY TYPE	KINDA COOL	A SOLID BOT	SO AWESOME!	BEST OF THE BEST

FAVORITE FEATURES:

BEST ADVANTAGE IN BATTLE:

This out-of-control robot blasts through the arena like a giant spinning top! As a circular full-body spinner, it needs the bar at the top to tell drivers which direction it is facing. This bar also helps the robot right itself when it's jostled in battle. Gigabyte's reliability in battle makes it a force to be reckoned with.

HOMETOWN: OCEANSIDE, CALIFORNIA

TYPE: FULL-BODIED SPINNER

TOTAL MATCHES: 22

WIN PERCENTAGE: 55%

WINS: 12

LOSSES: 10

KNOCKOUTS: 11

KO PERCENTAGE: 50%

AVERAGE KNOCKOUT TIME: 108 SECONDS

Sloping sides act like a wedge
to flip over opponents

Durable shell is designed
especially for vertical spinners

MEET THE TEAM

The Robotic Death Company is led by engineer John Mladenik. He's one of the most successful builders of full-body spinners, having competed with another heavyweight spinner called Megabyte. Both Gigabyte and Megabyte have made it to the Top 16.

FULL TEAM

Blair Lindberg, Brent Rieker, Camden Wallraff, Carol Williams, John Mladenik, Liz Mladenik, Matt Maxham, Melissa Mladenik, Micha Chewy Lebowitz, Mike Lindberg, Wendy Maxham

RATE THIS BOT!

☐	☐	☐	☐	☐
1	2	3	4	5
NOT MY TYPE	KINDA COOL	A SOLID BOT	SO AWESOME!	BEST OF THE BEST

FAVORITE FEATURES:

BEST ADVANTAGE IN BATTLE:

GRUFF

Meet a menacing robot that lifts and lights up! This six-wheeled box-wedge bot has steel lifting forks and two flamethrowers. The forks can lift up to 400 lbs with control and precision. The flamethrowers shoot 3000°F flames. That's a higher temperature than any other weapon in BattleBots history!

HOMETOWN: PALM HARBOR, FLORIDA

TYPE: LIFTER/GRAPPLER + TORCH

TOTAL MATCHES: 17

WIN PERCENTAGE: 41%

WINS: 7

LOSSES: 10

KNOCKOUTS: 5

KO PERCENTAGE: 29%

AVERAGE KNOCKOUT TIME: 106 SECONDS

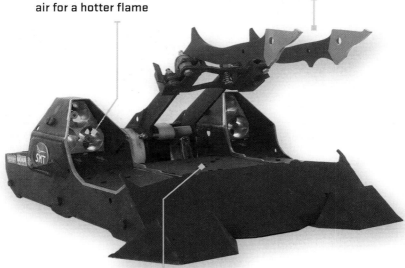

Torch nozzles suck in extra air for a hotter flame

Lifting forks are made from magnum triple-alloy steel

Drive system combines brushed motors and brushless motors

MEET THE TEAM

Sam McAmis is a teacher and the team captain of Team Gruff. He named their robot after "The Three Billy Goats Gruff," a fairy tale he enjoyed in his childhood. Sam also grew up around goats!

FULL TEAM

Chuck Butler, Hugh Savoldelli, Jason Rogers, Jason Ryan, Jeremy Butler, Marcello Mennone, Sam McAmis, Stephen Chapman, Vinny McAmis

RATE THIS BOT!

☐	☐	☐	☐	☐
1	2	3	4	5
NOT MY TYPE	KINDA COOL	A SOLID BOT	SO AWESOME!	BEST OF THE BEST

FAVORITE FEATURES:

BEST ADVANTAGE IN BATTLE:

HiJinx lives up to its name by starting all kinds of trouble in the BattleBox! This two-wheeled bot is the biggest horizontal spinner in the competition. It has an undercutting bar that is 48 inches long and spins up to 1,400 rpm. Watch out for this neon demon!

HOMETOWN: OAKLAND, CALIFORNIA

TYPE: BAR SPINNER (HORIZONTAL)

TOTAL MATCHES: 11

WIN PERCENTAGE: 45%

WINS: 5

LOSSES: 6

KNOCKOUTS: 4

KO PERCENTAGE: 36%

AVERAGE KNOCKOUT TIME: 101 SECONDS

Wheels are one inch thick and made from durable UHMW, a very tough plastic

Strong head and tail pieces provide stability

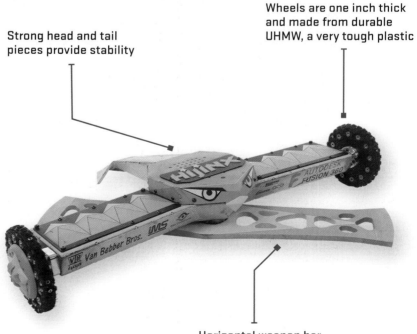

Horizontal weapon bar made of AR500 steel

MEET THE TEAM

Offbeat Robotics is led by Jen Herchenroeder, a skilled engineer and metalworker. Outside of BattleBots, she has competed with electric ride-on cars in Power Racing events. The team's lead engineer is Orion Beach, who has been building robots for over 20 years.

FULL TEAM

Chas Leichner, Chestley Couch, Jen Herchenroeder, Madeline Hagan, Matthew Garrett, Orion Beach, Paloma Juanita Fautley

RATE THIS BOT!

☐	☐	☐	☐	☐
1	**2**	**3**	**4**	**5**
NOT MY TYPE	KINDA COOL	A SOLID BOT	SO AWESOME!	BEST OF THE BEST

FAVORITE FEATURES:

BEST ADVANTAGE IN BATTLE:

When HUGE debuted in the BattleBox, crowds had never seen anything like it. This robot's ginormous size is due in part to massive wheels that are 40 inches in diameter. Its powerful spinning bar attacks from above to unleash full-on destruction. Win or lose, love or hate, HUGE always creates a spectacle!

HOMETOWN: SOUTH WINDSOR, CONNECTICUT

TYPE: BAR SPINNER (VERTICAL)

TOTAL MATCHES: 23

WIN PERCENTAGE: 52%

WINS: 12

LOSSES: 11

KNOCKOUTS: 5

KO PERCENTAGE: 23%

AVERAGE KNOCKOUT TIME: 125 SECONDS

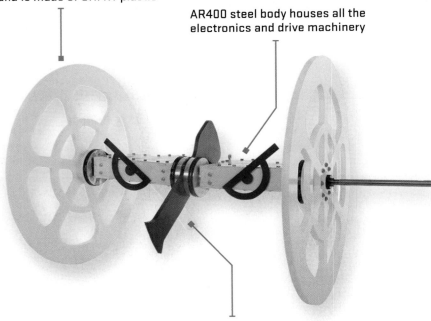

Each wheel weighs 30 lbs and is made of UHMW plastic

AR400 steel body houses all the electronics and drive machinery

Machine-cut stabilizing legs maintain balance and structural integrity

MEET THE TEAM

Team HUGE is a group of robot builders who come from all over the East Coast of the United States. Team captain Jonathan Schultz and fellow teammate Peter Lombardo were fresh out of college when they entered their first robotic combat competition and met the rest of their team while entering local competitions.

FULL TEAM

Don Doerfler, Garrett Santoline, Jonathan Schultz, Maddie Thumma, Peter Lombardo

RATE THIS BOT!

☐ 1	☐ 2	☐ 3	☐ 4	☐ 5
NOT MY TYPE	KINDA COOL	A SOLID BOT	SO AWESOME!	BEST OF THE BEST

FAVORITE FEATURES:

BEST ADVANTAGE IN BATTLE:

Hydra is a ruthless killer known for its brutality in combat. This robot's flipping arm uses hydraulics, which means it uses fluid to build up a lot of pressure. That pressure releases in a burst that has enough force to launch opponents into the ceiling! As a launcher and a lifter, Hydra is lethal.

HOMETOWN: DORCHESTER, WISCONSIN

TYPE: LAUNCHER

TOTAL MATCHES: 20

WIN PERCENTAGE: 75%

WINS: 15

LOSSES: 5

KNOCKOUTS: 10

KO PERCENTAGE: 50%

AVERAGE KNOCKOUT TIME: 105 SECONDS

The only hydraulic flipper ever used in the history of BattleBots

Flat, low-to-the-ground design helps it get underneath other bots

AR500 steel front plates offer strong defense

MEET THE TEAM

Hydra is another bot created by Team Whyachi Robotics, a lineup spearheaded by the Ewert family. The team has a large fan base, in part because of their tendency to talk a big game! Not everyone is a fan, though, thanks to their sometimes ruthless tactics in the arena.

FULL TEAM

Jake Ewert, Rachel "Tiny Hands" Stuplich, Richard "Dick" Stuplich

RATE THIS BOT!

☐	☐	☐	☐	☐
1	**2**	**3**	**4**	**5**
NOT MY TYPE	KINDA COOL	A SOLID BOT	SO AWESOME!	BEST OF THE BEST

FAVORITE FEATURES:

BEST ADVANTAGE IN BATTLE:

HYPERSHOCK

HyperShock might look like a race car, but it does so much more than drive around doing burnouts and doughnuts. (Although it can do those!) Its vertical spinner is a drum configured with two weapon discs for explosive hits and ultimate carnage. HyperShock will chew up and spit out anything that gets in its way.

HOMETOWN: MIAMI, FLORIDA

TYPE: DISC SPINNER (VERTICAL)

TOTAL MATCHES: 32

WIN PERCENTAGE: 53%

WINS: 17

LOSSES: 15

KNOCKOUTS: 15

KO PERCENTAGE: 47%

AVERAGE KNOCKOUT TIME: 88 SECONDS

Armor made of titanium, aluminum, and AR500 steel

Ears prevent the weapon from hitting the ground when upside down

Front wedge can be swapped out for hinged forks

MEET THE TEAM

Will Bales is the charismatic captain of Team HyperShock. He leads a team of engineers, designers, and technical specialists who have over 50 years of combined experience in robot combat. Every year that HyperShock has competed, the team has built the robot on-site right before filming!

FULL TEAM

Alexandra Bales, Collin Royster, Connie Ryan, Derek Deville, Gary Nguyen, Greg Bales, Isaac Lubarsky, Kat Cochran, Kyle Awner, Natalie Royster, Will Bales

RATE THIS BOT!

☐	☐	☐	☐	☐
1	2	3	4	5
NOT MY TYPE	KINDA COOL	A SOLID BOT	SO AWESOME!	BEST OF THE BEST

FAVORITE FEATURES:

BEST ADVANTAGE IN BATTLE:

Icewave was truly built for destruction. The spinning blade on top of this robot doesn't just inflict pain—it has literally sliced opponents in half! This primary weapon is driven by a gas-powered engine, which comes from a special saw that firefighters use. That's a lot of power!

HOMETOWN: BURLINGAME, CALIFORNIA

TYPE: BAR SPINNER (HORIZONTAL)

TOTAL MATCHES: 16

WIN PERCENTAGE: 50%

WINS: 8

LOSSES: 8

KNOCKOUTS: 7

KO PERCENTAGE: 44%

AVERAGE KNOCKOUT TIME: 53 SECONDS

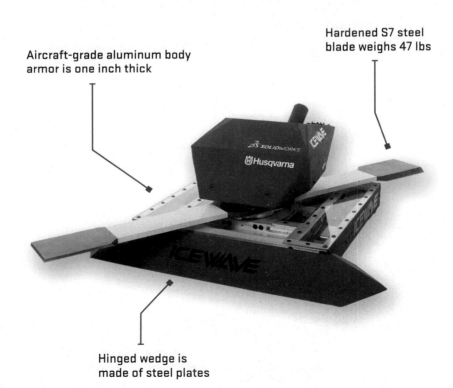

Aircraft-grade aluminum body armor is one inch thick

Hardened S7 steel blade weighs 47 lbs

Hinged wedge is made of steel plates

MEET THE TEAM

Marc DeVidts is a self-taught engineer who has been making combat robots since high school. He is the leader of Team Icewave and the driver of their killer bot. Marc is also the founder of a tech startup called Double Robotics.

FULL TEAM

Alex Espinosa, Angela Bamblett, Jamie Price, Marc DeVidts, Michael Macht, Michael Turner

RATE THIS BOT!

☐ 1 NOT MY TYPE	☐ 2 KINDA COOL	☐ 3 A SOLID BOT	☐ 4 SO AWESOME!	☐ 5 BEST OF THE BEST

FAVORITE FEATURES:

BEST ADVANTAGE IN BATTLE:

All bets are off when JackPot rolls into the arena. This casino-themed robot is armed with a dual-disc vertical spinner that knocks out opponents. The Double Die-monds spinners are mounted on a center core and can be swapped out for a single heart-shaped blade call the "Heartbreaker"!

HOMETOWN: LAS VEGAS, NEVADA

TYPE: DISC SPINNER (VERTICAL)

TOTAL MATCHES: 10

WIN PERCENTAGE: 60%

WINS: 6

LOSSES: 4

KNOCKOUTS: 5

KO PERCENTAGE: 50%

AVERAGE KNOCKOUT TIME: 81 SECONDS

Self-righting mechanism mounted in the back

AR500 steel frame to resist attack

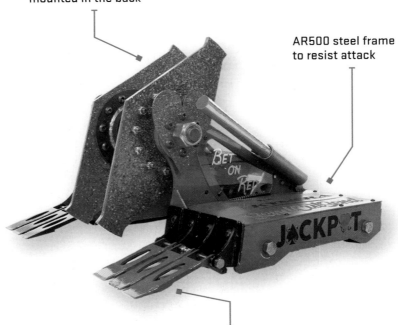

Hinged wedgelets at the front are designed to slide underneath opponents

MEET THE TEAM

Team VCR (Vegas Combat Robotics) is from Las Vegas, the casino capital of the world. They managed to build JackPot in just four weeks! Captain Jeff Waters is a plumber and pipe fitter who leads a stellar team of builders and engineers.

FULL TEAM

Jason Woods, Jeff Waters, Kat Waters, Lucas Grell, Robert Stehn, Shea Johns

RATE THIS BOT!

☐	☐	☐	☐	☐
1	**2**	**3**	**4**	**5**
NOT MY TYPE	KINDA COOL	A SOLID BOT	SO AWESOME!	BEST OF THE BEST

FAVORITE FEATURES:

BEST ADVANTAGE IN BATTLE:

In Scandinavian folklore, a kraken is a giant sea monster that strikes fear in the hearts of sailors. In the BattleBox, Kraken is a two-wheeled robot that strikes fear in the cogs and gears of its opponents! The signature crushing weapon uses an airbag to push the top jaw downward and crush other robots.

HOMETOWN: TITUSVILLE, FLORIDA

TYPE: CRUSHER

TOTAL MATCHES: 23

WIN PERCENTAGE: 26%

WINS: 6

LOSSES: 17

KNOCKOUTS: 0

KO PERCENTAGE: 0%

AVERAGE KNOCKOUT TIME: N/A

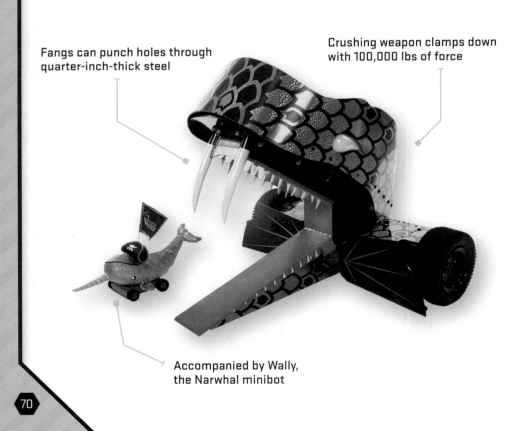

Fangs can punch holes through quarter-inch-thick steel

Crushing weapon clamps down with 100,000 lbs of force

Accompanied by Wally, the Narwhal minibot

MEET THE TEAM

CE Robots is a family team from Florida. The team captain is Matt Spurk, a rocket scientist who designed, engineered, and fabricated Kraken. He's competed in robotic combat battles for over 15 years. You can't miss them in the arena—the entire team always dresses like pirates!

FULL TEAM

Cayden Spurk, Ethan Spurk, John Summers, Matt Spurk, Michael Spurk, Peggy Spurk, Sara Spurk, Todd Garrett

RATE THIS BOT!

☐	☐	☐	☐	☐
1	**2**	**3**	**4**	**5**
NOT MY TYPE	KINDA COOL	A SOLID BOT	SO AWESOME!	BEST OF THE BEST

FAVORITE FEATURES:

BEST ADVANTAGE IN BATTLE:

This robot's jaws take a serious bite out of the competition! Lock-Jaw has a 45-lb vertical bar that spins with fury and ferocity. It's a resilient bot, too. If you flip Lock-Jaw over, the weapon modal free pivots to allow for complete four-wheel-drive invertibility.

HOMETOWN: SAN DIEGO, CALIFORNIA

TYPE: DISC SPINNER (VERTICAL)

TOTAL MATCHES: 32

WIN PERCENTAGE: 59%

WINS: 19

LOSSES: 13

KNOCKOUTS: 12

KO PERCENTAGE: 38%

AVERAGE KNOCKOUT TIME: 114 SECONDS

Stocky build at the front supports the weight of the weapon

45-lb vertical bar delivers crushing blows

Long, modular lower jaws articulate to upend opponents

MEET THE TEAM

Donald Hutson is the legendary builder of Lock-Jaw. He's one of the best in the sport, having competed for over 20 years and won many trophies along the way. Donald is the captain of Mutant Robots, an accomplished team of mechanical engineers based in Southern California.

FULL TEAM

Allie Levy, Donald Hutson, Dylan Walter, Johnny Media, Paul Ferrell, Reginald Wilson, Walter Maksimow

RATE THIS BOT!

☐	☐	☐	☐	☐
1	2	3	4	5
NOT MY TYPE	KINDA COOL	A SOLID BOT	SO AWESOME!	BEST OF THE BEST

FAVORITE FEATURES:

BEST ADVANTAGE IN BATTLE:

This robot has the agility, speed, and reflexes of a crazy killer cat. MaDCatTer is a supercharged machine, running on ten motors that are used for drive and powering a 48-lb vertical disc spinner. Compact and well engineered, MaDCatTer claws its way through the competition.

HOMETOWN: POMONA, CALIFORNIA

TYPE: DISC SPINNER (VERTICAL)

TOTAL MATCHES: 18

WIN PERCENTAGE: 61%

WINS: 11

LOSSES: 7

KNOCKOUTS: 10

KO PERCENTAGE: 56%

AVERAGE KNOCKOUT TIME: 76 SECONDS

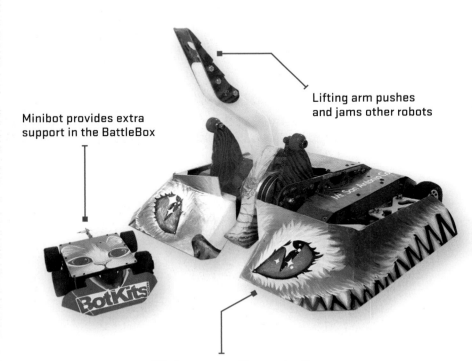

Minibot provides extra support in the BattleBox

Lifting arm pushes and jams other robots

Wedge armor offers protection from horizontal spinners

MEET THE TEAM

MaDCatTer was built by Martin Mason, a mad professor who teaches engineering and physics at Mt. San Antonio College. His team, Bad Kitty, is made up of current and past students. Martin's personality as a smack-talking professional wrestler makes him a fan favorite.

FULL TEAM

Allen Phuong, Calvin Iba, Martin Mason, Ryan Lau, Thomas Thomas

RATE THIS BOT!

☐	☐	☐	☐	☐
1	2	3	4	5
NOT MY TYPE	KINDA COOL	A SOLID BOT	SO AWESOME!	BEST OF THE BEST

FAVORITE FEATURES:

BEST ADVANTAGE IN BATTLE:

Malice is armed with one of the biggest disc spinners in the competition. This signature weapon is a giant 55-lb drumette that goes by the name Big Red. The weapon can be switched out depending on Malice's opponent. The other spinners' names are just as intimidating: Purple Pain, Drumstick, and Rolling Blackout.

HOMETOWN: SAN JOSE, CALIFORNIA

TYPE: HORIZONTAL DRUMETTE

TOTAL MATCHES: 13

WIN PERCENTAGE: 46%

WINS: 6

LOSSES: 7

KNOCKOUTS: 3

KO PERCENTAGE: 23%

AVERAGE KNOCKOUT TIME: 122 SECONDS

Specially designed rear helps prevent the robot from flipping over

Strong top armor protects against dangerous overhead weapons

Thick, flat design keeps it low to the ground and dominates floor space

MEET THE TEAM

Team Malice is led by Bunny Sauriol, who comes into battle wearing bunny ears on her head! She was a big fan of BattleBots, which inspired her to start building her own combat robot. Bunny is a passionate captain and brilliant strategist.

FULL TEAM

Bunny Sauriol, David Liaw, David Rush, David Small, Isaak Malers, Nick Dobrikov

RATE THIS BOT!				
☐	☐	☐	☐	☐
1	**2**	**3**	**4**	**5**
NOT MY TYPE	KINDA COOL	A SOLID BOT	SO AWESOME!	BEST OF THE BEST

FAVORITE FEATURES:

BEST ADVANTAGE IN BATTLE:

Just looking at Mammoth, you can see this is not your typical robot! This two-wheeled, triangular menace is changing the game. It's as tall as a refrigerator, and its massive rotating weapon can lift and catapult unwitting opponents. If you get in Mammoth's way, you will get launched!

HOMETOWN: BALTIMORE, MARYLAND

TYPE: ROTARY LIFTER

TOTAL MATCHES: 18

WIN PERCENTAGE: 39%

WINS: 7

LOSSES: 11

KNOCKOUTS: 5

KO PERCENTAGE: 28%

AVERAGE KNOCKOUT TIME: 96 SECONDS

Weapon motor has a peak load of over 185 horsepower

Front forks provide stability and create a catchment area that opponents drive into

Foam-filled tires are 13 inches tall

MEET THE TEAM

Ricky Willems is an electrical product designer who leads Team Mammoth. He was inspired to build his own robot after being a longtime fan of BattleBots. Ricky's enthusiasm for his team of engineers, fabricators, and artists is infectious!

FULL TEAM

Anna Goodridge, Brandon Young, Brice Farrell, Courtney Hollis, Liz Chavarria, Matt Bailey, Ricky Willems, Thuong "Lou" Nguyen

RATE THIS BOT!

☐	☐	☐	☐	☐
1	**2**	**3**	**4**	**5**
NOT MY TYPE	KINDA COOL	A SOLID BOT	SO AWESOME!	BEST OF THE BEST

FAVORITE FEATURES:

BEST ADVANTAGE IN BATTLE:

Minotaur is a big, bad beast from Brazil! Its primary weapon is a massive drum that spins exceptionally fast and stores a lot of energy. When Minotaur unleashes that energy, opponents get ripped to shreds. It's no wonder this robot has previously been awarded Most Destructive Robot!

HOMETOWN: RIO DE JANEIRO, BRAZIL

TYPE: DRUM SPINNER

TOTAL MATCHES: 27

WIN PERCENTAGE: 70%

WINS: 19

LOSSES: 8

KNOCKOUTS: 13

KO PERCENTAGE: 48%

AVERAGE KNOCKOUT TIME: 108 SECONDS

Tough armor made from very thick aluminum

Drum spins up to 10,000 rpm, the maximum allowed in competition

Wedges and wedgelets can be attached to either side of the drum

MEET THE TEAM

RioBotz hails from PUC-Rio, a university in Rio de Janeiro. The group was started by Professor Marco Antônio Meggiolaro, who earned a PhD from the Massachusetts Institute of Technology (MIT) and went on to build Minotaur. RioBotz is mostly made up of students with engineering and mechanic skills.

FULL TEAM

Carlos Junior, Daniel Freitas, David Steagall, Marco Antônio Meggiolaro, Marcos Angeli, Matheus Amaral, Vinicius Monteiro

RATE THIS BOT!

☐	☐	☐	☐	☐
1	**2**	**3**	**4**	**5**
NOT MY TYPE	KINDA COOL	A SOLID BOT	SO AWESOME!	BEST OF THE BEST

FAVORITE FEATURES:

BEST ADVANTAGE IN BATTLE:

This robot was built in Britain, and its blade is the biggest, fastest vertical spinner in the United Kingdom! When Monsoon fights stateside, it comes armed with many different armor setups, fork attachments, and weapon blades. The word "monsoon" means rainy season, and this robot lives up to its name by bringing the thunder in battle and raining down the pain!

HOMETOWN: TURVEY, UNITED KINGDOM

TYPE: BAR SPINNER (VERTICAL)

TOTAL MATCHES: 11

WIN PERCENTAGE: 55%

WINS: 6

LOSSES: 5

KNOCKOUTS: 3

KO PERCENTAGE: 27%

AVERAGE KNOCKOUT TIME: 67 SECONDS

Forks at the top and bottom help feed opponents into the spinner

Armor plates can be switched out depending on the opponent

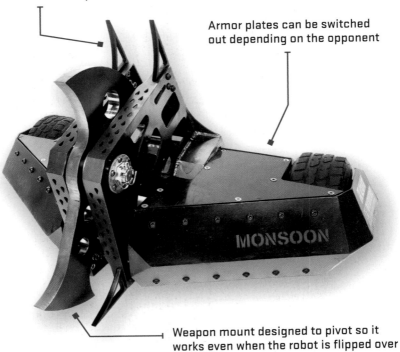

Weapon mount designed to pivot so it works even when the robot is flipped over

MEET THE TEAM

UK based Team Monsoon has competed all over the world. They also build smaller robots to fight in different weight classes, including Drizzle and Straddle. Their captain, Tom Brewster, is a design engineer for a power electronics company. His interest in combat robotics gave him the experience needed to pursue his career as an engineer, after originally working in the video game industry.

FULL TEAM

David Griffin, Rory Mangles, Tim "Rackers" Rackley, Sarah Asplin, Tom Brewster

RATE THIS BOT!

☐	☐	☐	☐	☐
1	**2**	**3**	**4**	**5**
NOT MY TYPE	KINDA COOL	A SOLID BOT	SO AWESOME!	BEST OF THE BEST

FAVORITE FEATURES:

BEST ADVANTAGE IN BATTLE:

PERFECT PHOENIX

When the overhead bar on Perfect Phoenix builds up to speed, it will slice anything that crosses its path! In mythology, a phoenix is a bird that bursts into flames, then rises from the ashes with renewed life. Like its namesake, Perfect Phoenix takes the heat and just keeps coming back for more!

HOMETOWN: HERNDON, VIRGINIA

TYPE: BAR SPINNER (HORIZONTAL)

TOTAL MATCHES: 7

WIN PERCENTAGE: 43%

WINS: 3

LOSSES: 4

KNOCKOUTS: 1

KO PERCENTAGE: 14%

AVERAGE KNOCKOUT TIME: 59 SECONDS

Frame is reinforced with steel to withstand impact

Weapon is powered by two automotive motors

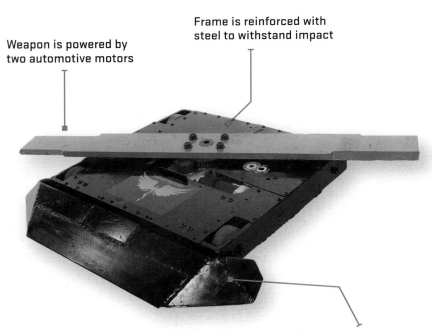

Wedge helps prevent contact with other opponents' weapons

MEET THE TEAM

Tyler Nguyen is the youngest team captain in the history of BattleBots. He was 11 years old when he debuted as Perfect Phoenix's driver, and his incredible maneuvering behind the controller secured a knockout win in its first-ever battle. Read more about Tyler on page 122.

FULL TEAM

Juli Johnson, Scottie Riddle, Tyler Nguyen

RATE THIS BOT!

☐	☐	☐	☐	☐
1	2	3	4	5
NOT MY TYPE	KINDA COOL	A SOLID BOT	SO AWESOME!	BEST OF THE BEST

FAVORITE FEATURES:

BEST ADVANTAGE IN BATTLE:

Make way for the mean green fighting machine! This fierce frog stays ahead of the competition by switching up its configuration for every match. As a modular robot, it can change its weapon to take advantage of each opponent's weaknesses. The weapons are primarily savage spinners, including an undercutter and two types of vertical spinners.

HOMETOWN: WORCESTER, MASSACHUSETTS

TYPE: MODULAR

TOTAL MATCHES: 20

WIN PERCENTAGE: 70%

WINS: 14

LOSSES: 6

KNOCKOUTS: 13

KO PERCENTAGE: 65%

AVERAGE KNOCKOUT TIME: 94 SECONDS

Molded top armor defends against nothing, but has a froggy look

Highest voltage weapon system in BattleBots history, reaching 252 volts

Undercutting disc weighs a hefty 50 lbs

MEET THE TEAM

The team behind Ribbot is made up of students and alumni from Worcester Polytechnic Institute (WPI). Their captain is David Jin, who was the president of the WPI Robotics Club. Outside of BattleBots, David and the rest of the team compete in local events in smaller weight classes.

FULL TEAM

Alex Johnson, Andrew Mularoni, Christian Cooper, David Jin, Hector the Frog, Lucas Buermeyer, Nick Hom, Nick Sorensen, Tim Bell, Zeke Andreassen

RATE THIS BOT!

☐	☐	☐	☐	☐
1	**2**	**3**	**4**	**5**
NOT MY TYPE	KINDA COOL	A SOLID BOT	SO AWESOME!	BEST OF THE BEST

FAVORITE FEATURES:

BEST ADVANTAGE IN BATTLE:

ROTATOR

Rotator is durable and destructive, equipped with deadly discs that deliver devastation. This robot is armed with a single horizontal spinner, but the blade can be switched out for different fights. Rotator's ability to dismantle opponents in the BattleBox has led to the distinction of a Most Destructive Robot award!

HOMETOWN: MIAMI, FLORIDA

TYPE: BAR SPINNER (HORIZONTAL)

TOTAL MATCHES: 26

WIN PERCENTAGE: 62%

WINS: 16

LOSSES: 10

KNOCKOUTS: 8

KO PERCENTAGE: 31%

AVERAGE KNOCKOUT TIME: 105 SECONDS

Brushless motors provide more power for less weight

Wheel guards specially designed to protect tires

Bar spinner can be mounted to the top

MEET THE TEAM

Team Revolution is always dressed to impress. To match their shiny gold robot, they wear black-and-gold clothing head to toe and sport light-up gold sneakers. This flashy bunch is led by Victor Soto, a robotics systems engineer who has 20 years of experience in robot combat.

FULL TEAM

Ali Tariq, Carl Gayle, Jordan Sangerman, Mark Palm, Victor Soto

RATE THIS BOT!				
☐	☐	☐	☐	☐
1	2	3	4	5
NOT MY TYPE	KINDA COOL	A SOLID BOT	SO AWESOME!	BEST OF THE BEST

FAVORITE FEATURES:

BEST ADVANTAGE IN BATTLE:

Rusty might be one of the newer competitors in BattleBots, but this robot isn't a noob! It came out of nowhere in its debut season to defeat veteran bots and score some upset victories. Although it might look unassuming with its rusted coat and domed head, Rusty has sledgehammer and jackhammer weapons that are powerful punishers.

HOMETOWN: ANTIOCH, ILLINOIS

TYPE: HAMMER

TOTAL MATCHES: 7

WIN PERCENTAGE: 29%

WINS: 2

LOSSES: 5

KNOCKOUTS: 1

KO PERCENTAGE: 14%

AVERAGE KNOCKOUT TIME: 132 SECONDS

Original domed head was made from a kitchen bowl

Pneumatic spike weapon pounds like a jackhammer

Runs on long rubber tracks, protected by cage-style tread guards

MEET THE TEAM

Team Iron Force is a one-man team! Dave Eaton is the mechanical engineer who built Rusty and drives him in the arena. Rusty and Dave have quickly become fan favorites. They won the Rookie of the Year award after their first season.

FULL TEAM
David Eaton

RATE THIS BOT!

☐	☐	☐	☐	☐
1	**2**	**3**	**4**	**5**
NOT MY TYPE	KINDA COOL	A SOLID BOT	SO AWESOME!	BEST OF THE BEST

FAVORITE FEATURES:

BEST ADVANTAGE IN BATTLE:

SawBlaze is a brutal bully in the BattleBox and one of the fiercest robots in the competition. Its signature weapon is a "hammer saw," a giant spinning blade mounted to the end of an arm, which hammers down with unapologetic force. As if that isn't enough, a flamethrower is mounted to the front to roast opponents in a blaze of fury!

HOMETOWN: CAMBRIDGE, MASSACHUSETTS

TYPE: HAMMER SAW, CUTTING SAW, FLAMETHROWER

TOTAL MATCHES: 26

WIN PERCENTAGE: 65%

WINS: 17

LOSSES: 9

KNOCKOUTS: 6

KO PERCENTAGE: 23%

AVERAGE KNOCKOUT TIME: 135 SECONDS

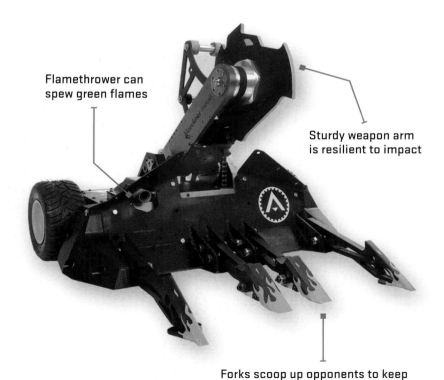

Flamethrower can spew green flames

Sturdy weapon arm is resilient to impact

Forks scoop up opponents to keep them in place for brutal hammering

MEET THE TEAM

MIT graduate Jamison Go is the captain of Team SawBlaze. He has spent thousands of hours perfecting SawBlaze. The team is a diverse group of people who are spread all over the country. Its members span five states and four time zones!

FULL TEAM

Jake Chesin, Jamison Go, John Mayo, Lucy Du, Raymond Ma, Samantha Glassner, Shakti Shaligram, Stephanie Chesin

RATE THIS BOT!

☐	☐	☐	☐	☐
1	2	3	4	5
NOT MY TYPE	KINDA COOL	A SOLID BOT	SO AWESOME!	BEST OF THE BEST

FAVORITE FEATURES:

BEST ADVANTAGE IN BATTLE:

When this mechanical shark goes into battle, it's a feeding frenzy! Sharko is almost eight feet long with a tail that whips and lashes uncontrollably. Its giant jaws chomp and clamp down to reduce opponents to chum. Sharko's original design was made of recycled parts, but it has since evolved into a sleek slayer.

HOMETOWN: SONORA

TYPE: GRAPPLER

TOTAL MATCHES: 7

WIN PERCENTAGE: 29%

WINS: 2

LOSSES: 5

KNOCKOUTS: 1

KO PERCENTAGE: 14%

AVERAGE KNOCKOUT TIME: 142 SECONDS

Plated armor adds a strong layer of defense

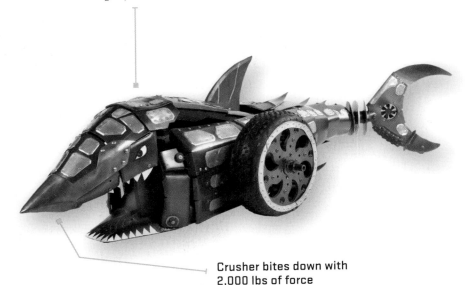

Crusher bites down with 2,000 lbs of force

MEET THE TEAM

Team Aquatic Machine Force has been building and competing with combat robots for 20 years. Edward Robinson is their iconic captain. Before building bots and starting his own combat robotics league, he swallowed swords and breathed fire in the circus!

FULL TEAM

Dominic Borg, Edward Robinson, Zach Hassanein

RATE THIS BOT!

☐	☐	☐	☐	☐
1	**2**	**3**	**4**	**5**
NOT MY TYPE	KINDA COOL	A SOLID BOT	SO AWESOME!	BEST OF THE BEST

FAVORITE FEATURES:

BEST ADVANTAGE IN BATTLE:

Shatter! might look like a sparkly disco ball, but it's definitely NOT a party decoration. This vicious robot has two different hammer attachments designed for incredible reach and deadly precision. One is called the Mary Special, a double-edged hammer with sharp slicing edges. The other is a shock-mounted hammer used to combat spinners known as New Rusty.

HOMETOWN: BROOKLYN, NEW YORK

TYPE: HAMMER/SWORD

TOTAL MATCHES: 15

WIN PERCENTAGE: 60%

WINS: 9

LOSSES: 6

KNOCKOUTS: 3

KO PERCENTAGE: 20%

AVERAGE KNOCKOUT TIME: 102 SECONDS

Serrated saw-like edges snag opponents' belts and chains

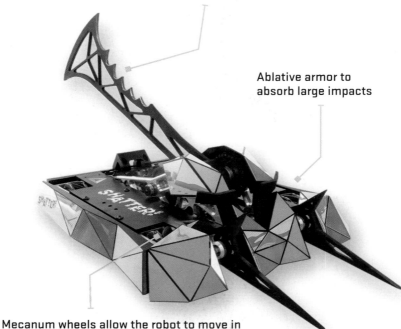

Ablative armor to absorb large impacts

Mecanum wheels allow the robot to move in any direction and always face its opponent

MEET THE TEAM

BotsFC is an up-and-coming team on the BattleBots scene. Their captain is Adam Wrigley, a mechanical engineer who aims to push the boundaries of robot combat. Not only have they competed in the United States, but they've also taken their hammer skills to tournaments in China.

FULL TEAM

Adam Wrigley, Eric Wrigley, Mary Chimenti, Paul Gancitano

RATE THIS BOT!

☐	☐	☐	☐	☐
1	2	3	4	5
NOT MY TYPE	KINDA COOL	A SOLID BOT	SO AWESOME!	BEST OF THE BEST

FAVORITE FEATURES:

BEST ADVANTAGE IN BATTLE:

Skorpios is the robot with weapons galore! Its articulating arm has a range of different attachments for overhead attacks. Among the artillery is a 14-lb disc called T. rex and a 7-lb bar with sharp teeth called the Klondike Bar. When Skorpios is armed with the lighter weapon, it packs on more armor to make up the weight. That's smart strategy!

HOMETOWN: MORAGA, CALIFORNIA

TYPE: HAMMER SAW

TOTAL MATCHES: 28

WIN PERCENTAGE: 57%

WINS: 16

LOSSES: 12

KNOCKOUTS: 5

KO PERCENTAGE: 18%

AVERAGE KNOCKOUT TIME: 149 SECONDS

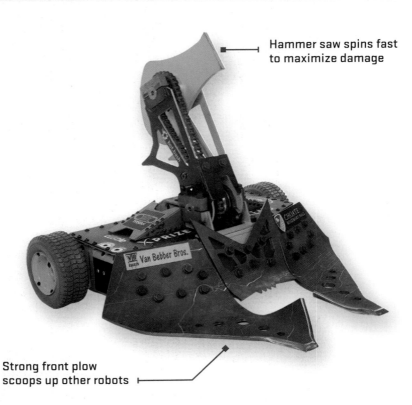

Hammer saw spins fast to maximize damage

Strong front plow scoops up other robots

MEET THE TEAM

When Bot Bash Party Crew isn't building combat robots and competing in tournaments, they organize parties and camps where kids learn how to make robots. Zachary Lytle is the team captain—he's also a professional yo-yo champion!

FULL TEAM

Allan Cecil, Ben Shafton, Bennett Funk, Dan Chatterton, Diana Tarlson, Leslie Shafton, Rob Wisecarver, Shannon Tobin, Tony Woodward, Will Prater, Zachary Lytle

RATE THIS BOT!

☐	☐	☐	☐	☐
1	**2**	**3**	**4**	**5**
NOT MY TYPE	KINDA COOL	A SOLID BOT	SO AWESOME!	BEST OF THE BEST

FAVORITE FEATURES:

BEST ADVANTAGE IN BATTLE

Nope, that name isn't a typo. It's a deliberately wiiiide moniker for a really wiiiide robot—14 feet wide, to be exact! The unique design of this robot allows it to wrap around opponents and render them defenseless. Wheeled modules on either side house the drive and weapon motors, as well as the electronics.

HOMETOWN: NEW YORK, NEW YORK

TYPE: GRAPPLER

TOTAL MATCHES: 8

WIN PERCENTAGE: 38%

WINS: 3

LOSSES: 5

KNOCKOUTS: 2

KO PERCENTAGE: 25%

AVERAGE KNOCKOUT TIME: 134 SECONDS

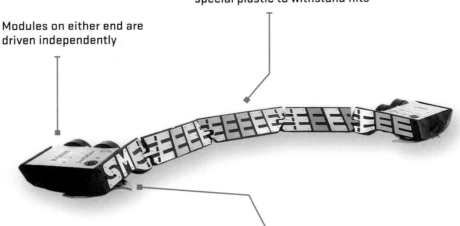

Wedge segments made with special plastic to withstand hits

Modules on either end are driven independently

AR500 steel undercutters cause serious damage

MEET THE TEAM

Joseph Fabiani is the brains behind SMEEEEEEEEEEEEEEEEEE. He's an industrial designer from New York City. Outside of BattleBots, he has built and driven other combat robots for competitions in the United States and China.

TEAM MEMBERS

Brandon Unger, Joseph Fabiani, Mark Fabiani, Zijing Ying

RATE THIS BOT!

☐	☐	☐	☐	☐
1	**2**	**3**	**4**	**5**
NOT MY TYPE	KINDA COOL	A SOLID BOT	SO AWESOME!	BEST OF THE BEST

FAVORITE FEATURES:

BEST ADVANTAGE IN BATTLE:

Bow down to one of the greats! Son of Whyachi is a performer with pedigree, a legendary fighter that built a legacy of knockdowns and knockouts. Over the years, its design has been modified for maximum aggression, but one thing has always remained: an iconic tribar weapon, which ultimately weighs a whopping 120 lbs!

HOMETOWN: DORCHESTER, WISCONSIN

TYPE: CAGED TRIBAR SPINNER

TOTAL MATCHES: 15

WIN PERCENTAGE: 60%

WINS: 9

LOSSES: 6

KNOCKOUTS: 9

KO PERCENTAGE: 60%

AVERAGE KNOCKOUT TIME: 77 SECONDS

Tribar weapon spins up to 190 mph to devastate opponents

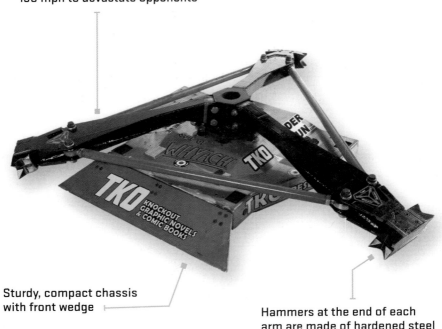

Sturdy, compact chassis with front wedge

Hammers at the end of each arm are made of hardened steel

MEET THE TEAM

The Ewert family from Wisconsin is the team behind Son of Whyachi. This group of builders came up with the word "whyachi"— it means "to inflict pain or damage." Although Son of Whyachi has retired, the family now competes with their latest robots, Fusion and Hydra (see more on pages 50 and 62).

FULL TEAM

Jake Ewert, Luke Ewert, Reese "Eeyore" Ewert, Richard "Dick" Stuplich, Terry Ewert

RATE THIS BOT!

☐ 1	☐ 2	☐ 3	☐ 4	☐ 5
NOT MY TYPE	KINDA COOL	A SOLID BOT	SO AWESOME!	BEST OF THE BEST

FAVORITE FEATURES:

BEST ADVANTAGE IN BATTLE:

SUBZERO

Robots don't get any *cooler* than SubZero! And one of the coolest things about this four-wheeled fighter is its mighty flipper. This pneumatic arm launches opponents into the air and tosses them around the arena. SubZero has won fights by knockout after sending victims flying into the air, only for them to come crashing down to their doom.

HOMETOWN: DALLAS, TEXAS

TYPE: FLIPPER

TOTAL MATCHES: 21

WIN PERCENTAGE: 33%

WINS: 7

LOSSES: 14

KNOCKOUTS: 7

KO PERCENTAGE: 33%

AVERAGE KNOCKOUT TIME: 95 SECONDS

Bulletproof top armor
protects the machinery

Front wedges scoop
opponents into the flipper

MEET THE TEAM

TeamXD started out as a father-and-son duo. Logan Davis began building combat robots with his dad, Brady, when he was 13 years old. Outside of BattleBots, Logan has competed in robot combat tournaments in China!

FULL TEAM

Brian Bray, Brady Davis, David Baker, Kris Mitchell, Logan Davis, Mitch Cerroni

RATE THIS BOT!

☐	☐	☐	☐	☐
1	**2**	**3**	**4**	**5**
NOT MY TYPE	KINDA COOL	A SOLID BOT	SO AWESOME!	BEST OF THE BEST

FAVORITE FEATURES:

BEST ADVANTAGE IN BATTLE:

This robot really packs a punch with its unique weapon. Tantrum's "puncher" is a spinning disc that moves back and forth on a rail system. When the disc is pulled back, it is protected from contact. But when the time is right, it can launch forward to punch an opponent that gets too close! Tantrum became BattleBots' World Champion in 2021, beating Witch Doctor in the Final to win the Giant Nut.

HOMETOWN: SAN DIEGO, CALIFORNIA, AND CAMBRIDGE, MASSACHUSETTS

TYPE: PUNCHER

TOTAL MATCHES: 24

WIN PERCENTAGE: 71%

WINS: 17

LOSSES: 7

KNOCKOUTS: 8

KO PERCENTAGE: 33%

AVERAGE KNOCKOUT TIME: 130 SECONDS

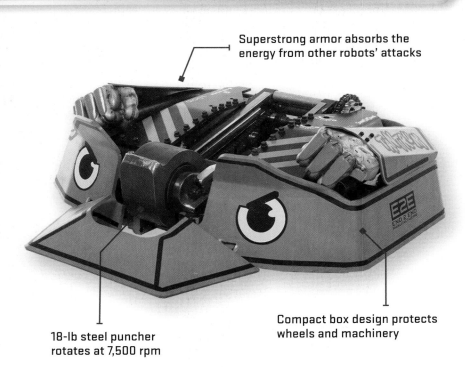

Superstrong armor absorbs the energy from other robots' attacks

18-lb steel puncher rotates at 7,500 rpm

Compact box design protects wheels and machinery

MEET THE TEAM

Tantrum was built by Seems Reasonable Robotics. The team captains are Alex Grant and Ginger Schmidt; driver Dillon Carey has been driving robots for over 15 years. Seems Reasonable is also the team behind Blip! (See page 26.)

FULL TEAM

Alec Kochis, Alex Grant, Aren Hill, Brian Silverman, Bryan Culver, David Mintz, Dillon Carey, Erica Chin, Ginger Schmidt, James Doherty, Jason Weihman, Katie Widen, Kristine Atiyeh, Max Chang, Sean Doherty, Steven Silverman, Sue Doherty, Will Stanley, Zach Marks

RATE THIS BOT!

☐ 1	☐ 2	☐ 3	☐ 4	☐ 5
NOT MY TYPE	KINDA COOL	A SOLID BOT	SO AWESOME!	BEST OF THE BEST

FAVORITE FEATURES:

BEST ADVANTAGE IN BATTLE:

TOMBSTONE

This heavyweight champion is one of the most successful bots in the competition. Tombstone blazes a path of destruction that has led all the way to winning the Giant Nut (in 2016)! Its weapon is a huge spinning bar with enough weight and speed to destroy opponents in seconds. Ouch!

HOMETOWN: PLACERVILLE, CALIFORNIA

TYPE: BAR SPINNER (HORIZONTAL)

TOTAL MATCHES: 34

WIN PERCENTAGE: 71%

WINS: 24

LOSSES: 10

KNOCKOUTS: 19

KO PERCENTAGE: 56%

AVERAGE KNOCKOUT TIME: 69 SECONDS

Special motors turbocharge the weapon with incredible spin-up speed

Primary weapon isn't just for attack—it protects the whole front of the robot

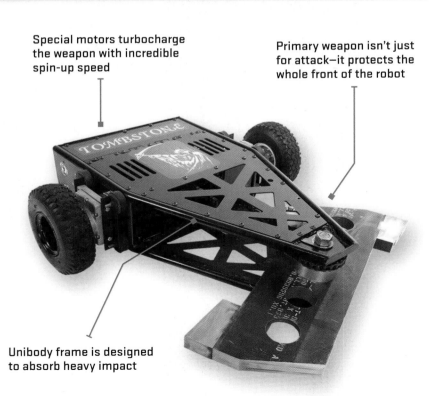

Unibody frame is designed to absorb heavy impact

MEET THE TEAM

Hardcore Robotics is one of the most feared teams in BattleBots. Ray Billings is the team captain, lead designer, and fabricator. He also worked as a prison guard for 12 years. His son, Justin Billings, joined the team when he was only 13 years old!

FULL TEAM

Kevin Benisi, Teri Billings, Justin Billings, Ray Billings, Lorna West, Rick Russ

RATE THIS BOT!

☐	☐	☐	☐	☐
1	**2**	**3**	**4**	**5**
NOT MY TYPE	KINDA COOL	A SOLID BOT	SO AWESOME!	BEST OF THE BEST

FAVORITE FEATURES:

BEST ADVANTAGE IN BATTLE:

UPPERCUT

Uppercut is the boxing bot with a fist of fury! Its primary weapon is an asymmetrical vertical spinning bar called "the fist"—one end is shaped like a puncher, while the other is curved to counterbalance it. The puncher weighs 50 lbs and can reach speeds of 200 mph. That's one mighty wallop!

HOMETOWN: CAMBRIDGE, MASSACHUSETTS

TYPE: PUNCHER

TOTAL MATCHES: 17

WIN PERCENTAGE: 71%

WINS: 12

LOSSES: 5

KNOCKOUTS: 11

KO PERCENTAGE: 65%

AVERAGE KNOCKOUT TIME: 77 SECONDS

Fist pops out, giving the weapon more reach than others in the competition

Puncher can be switched out for other weapons, including a 50-lb bar spinner

Curved front works as a plow to deflect opponents and guide them into the weapon

MEET THE TEAM

Team Uppercut is a talented group of students and alumni from MIT who make combat robots of all shapes and sizes. They've built everything from 1-lb bots to 250-lb heavyweight monsters. Team captain Alex Hattori is a recent graduate in mechanical engineering—he also wins yo-yo competitions!

FULL TEAM

Aaron Sliski, Alex Hattori, Anna Zolnikov, Austin Brown, Devansh Agrawal, Greg Xie, Jackson Gray, Jared DiCarlo, Jen Curtiss, Jeremy Germita, Jonhenry Poss, Jules Ferguson, Linda Hattori, Mason Massie, Saba Zerefa, Tiffany Hattori

RATE THIS BOT!

☐ 1 NOT MY TYPE	☐ 2 KINDA COOL	☐ 3 A SOLID BOT	☐ 4 SO AWESOME!	☐ 5 BEST OF THE BEST

FAVORITE FEATURES:

BEST ADVANTAGE IN BATTLE:

This well-driven bot has been optimized for control and maneuverability. Its spinning undercutter blade is designed to slice through wheels and target the undercarriage of its opponents. Valkyrie has different weapon options and multiple styles of armor that can be adapted to exploit opponents' weaknesses!

HOMETOWN: SOMERVILLE, MASSACHUSETTS

TYPE: DISC SPINNER (HORIZONTAL)

TOTAL MATCHES: 26

WIN PERCENTAGE: 62%

WINS: 16

LOSSES: 10

KNOCKOUTS: 11

KO PERCENTAGE: 42%

AVERAGE KNOCKOUT TIME: 91 SECONDS

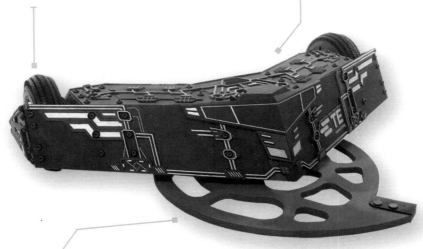

Titanium and steel armor protect the inner machinery

Drives up to 15 mph, which means it can cross the BattleBox in under four seconds

65-lb blade spins low to the ground at 250 mph

MEET THE TEAM

Questionable Designs has over 15 years of combined robot experience. Leanne Cushing is the fearless captain. Her expertise as a mechanical engineer has led this team of engineers and fabricators through devastating upsets and stunning victories.

FULL TEAM

Alexander Crease, Amanda Fowler, Bradley Roan, Daniel Gonzalez, Frederick Moore, Leanne Cushing, Lucas Ewing

RATE THIS BOT!				
☐	☐	☐	☐	☐
1	**2**	**3**	**4**	**5**
NOT MY TYPE	KINDA COOL	A SOLID BOT	SO AWESOME!	BEST OF THE BEST

FAVORITE FEATURES:

BEST ADVANTAGE IN BATTLE:

Meet one of the toughest bots in the competition! Whiplash is driven around the arena with surgical precision and strategically bashes and tosses bots into oblivion. Its main weapon is an aggressive spinning disc mounted on an arm that can rotate 180 degrees. This means it's super versatile because the arm works as a deadly lifter, while the disc can attack from above!

HOMETOWN: THOUSAND OAKS, CALIFORNIA

TYPE: ARTICULATED LIFTER/DISC SPINNER (VERTICAL)

TOTAL MATCHES: 31

WIN PERCENTAGE: 71%

WINS: 22

LOSSES: 9

KNOCKOUTS: 10

KO PERCENTAGE: 32%

AVERAGE KNOCKOUT TIME: 103 SECONDS

Disc spinner can be removed to free up weight for extra armor

Four-wheel drive designed for precise maneuvering

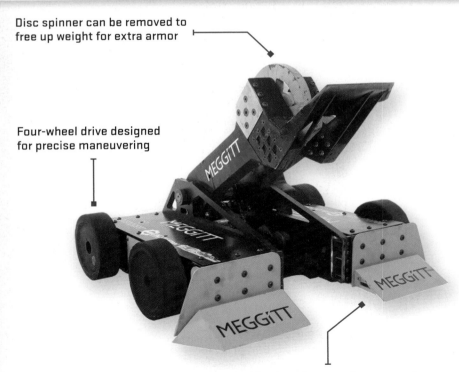

Front wedges can be swapped out for hinged forks, hinged wedgelets, or a flat plow

MEET THE TEAM

Fast Electric Robots is made up of the Vasquez family. Outside of BattleBots, they build and operate robots for TV shows! Matthew Vasquez is the team captain and driver. He's an electromechanical engineering student at Cal Poly Pomona, and he's renowned as the best driver in the competition.

FULL TEAM

Debbie Vasquez, Jason Vasquez, Jeff Vasquez, Matthew Vasquez

RATE THIS BOT!

☐ 1	☐ 2	☐ 3	☐ 4	☐ 5
NOT MY TYPE	KINDA COOL	A SOLID BOT	SO AWESOME!	BEST OF THE BEST

FAVORITE FEATURES:

BEST ADVANTAGE IN BATTLE:

The doctor is in! Witch Doctor isn't just spooky looking—it's spookily ferocious! This fan-favorite robot is armed with spinning vertical discs that destroy opponents. Its strength in the arena has allowed it to go all the way to the finals, twice nearly winning the Giant Nut.

HOMETOWN: MIAMI, FLORIDA

TYPE: DISC SPINNER (VERTICAL)

TOTAL MATCHES: 40

WIN PERCENTAGE: 65%

WINS: 26

LOSSES: 14

KNOCKOUTS: 19

KO PERCENTAGE: 48%

AVERAGE KNOCKOUT TIME: 94 SECONDS

Sophisticated motor assembly keeps weapon spinning while upside down

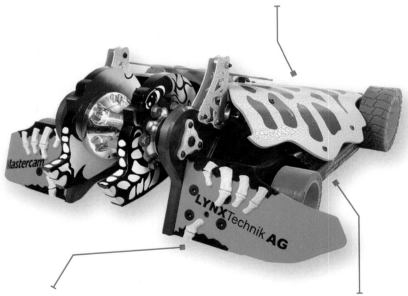

Front wedges push opponents while also protecting front wheels

Long wheelbase makes it harder to flip the robot

MEET THE TEAM

Andrea Gellatly is the captain of Team Witch Doctor. She started getting into robotics when she was in high school. Her husband, Mike, is a fellow team member. When they're in the arena, Mike drives their robot and Andrea is the weapons operator.

TEAM MEMBERS

Andrea Gellatly, Andrew Rudolph, Christian Chiriboga, Katheryn Sharp, Kurtis Wanner, Mike Gellatly, Paul Grata, Rick Pease, Steven Sharp

RATE THIS BOT!

☐ 1 NOT MY TYPE	☐ 2 KINDA COOL	☐ 3 A SOLID BOT	☐ 4 SO AWESOME!	☐ 5 BEST OF THE BEST

FAVORITE FEATURES:

BEST ADVANTAGE IN BATTLE:

Beware the Yeti! This robotic beast is a compact killer. Its main weapon is a massive 40-lb spinning drum that hits with devastating force. Yeti is so powerful that it's one of the few robots in BattleBots history that has defeated its opponent in a one-hit knockout.

HOMETOWN: SAN LUIS OBISPO, CALIFORNIA

TYPE: DRUM SPINNER

TOTAL MATCHES: 20

WIN PERCENTAGE: 65%

WINS: 13

LOSSES: 7

KNOCKOUTS: 8

KO PERCENTAGE: 40%

AVERAGE KNOCKOUT TIME: 112 SECONDS

Long, sharp lifting forks can retract into slots on the top panel

Large front wheels clamber over opponents

Drum picks up speed to spin up to 4,000 rpm

MEET THE TEAM

Yeti is co-captained by Greg Gibson and Christian Carlberg from C2 Robotics. Greg originally built Yeti and later teamed up with Christian, who has competed with other robots. Greg was 16 years old when he first saw Christian on BattleBots. Little did he know they would be building and driving robots together!

TEAM MEMBERS

Greg Gibson, Ange Santaguida, Christian Carlberg, James Arluck, Joe Sena

RATE THIS BOT!

☐	☐	☐	☐	☐
1	**2**	**3**	**4**	**5**
NOT MY TYPE	KINDA COOL	A SOLID BOT	SO AWESOME!	BEST OF THE BEST

FAVORITE FEATURES:

BEST ADVANTAGE IN BATTLE:

Drum roll, please! Here are some of the biggest, baddest, bravest bots in BattleBots history. These exemplary fighters have racked up some astounding records and achievements.

WINNINGEST BOT

BITE FORCE
Bite Force has won 96 percent of its matches!

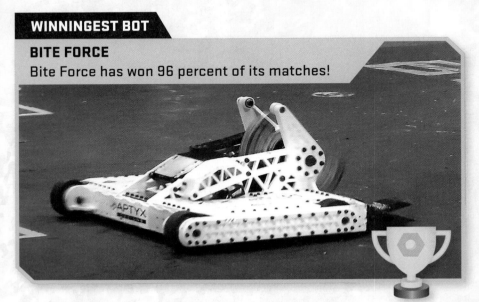

MOST DESTRUCTIVE BOT

TOMBSTONE
Tombstone has won the most fights by knockout! It has won by KO 19 times.

LARGEST BOT

MAMMOTH

There is no maximum size limit in BattleBots, so long as the robot fits within the square at the start of the match. Mammoth has used up ALL that space to become the largest heavyweight bot ever built, measuring 8 feet 9 inches long, 5 feet 4 inches wide, and 6 feet 3 inches tall.

FASTEST KNOCKOUT TIME

BLADE

The average time it takes Blade to knock out an opponent is 40 seconds!

MOST MATCHES

WITCH DOCTOR

With 40 matches under its belt, Witch Doctor has participated in the most fights. What a trouper!

As the sport of robot combat continues to evolve, the builders and bots have changed with it. Check out these groundbreakers who have pushed boundaries and changed the game.

KIDS RULE!

Ever since Tyler Nguyen discovered the sport of combat robotics at age 5, he couldn't wait to compete. He wouldn't have to wait too long! Tyler was only 11 years old when he became the youngest team captain in the history of BattleBots.

TYLER AND PERFECT PHOENIX

PRIDE IN THE BATTLEBOX

Lilith Specht is the first trans woman team captain in BattleBots. Lilith's robot, Sporkinok, is pink, blue, and white to represent the colors of the transgender pride flag. The team aims to inspire other LGBTQ+ people in the fields of robotics, STEM, and beyond!

LILITH AND SPORKINOK

AI OR DIE!

Artificial intelligence isn't just for robots in sci-fi movies. Chomp is an AI-powered bot that uses high-tech smarts in the BattleBox! It has a time-of-flight ranging sensor that maps the opponent's location in battle. A small computer under its armor can calculate the right time to strike its weapon.

CHOMP AND THE MACHINE CORPS

BIRTH OF THE LAUNCHER

When Bronco's explosive launcher debuted in the arena, it paved the way for a new type of battle. While most robots relied on spinners as their main weapons, Bronco and other Inertia Labs robots were the first to use pneumatic systems to create enough force to actually launch their opponents into the air. This innovation has since inspired many builders and their designs, and there are now several different types of launcher mechanisms in the competition.

BRONCO AND DUCK!

DESIGN YOUR OWN BATTLEBOT

Have you got what it takes to build your own bot? (Spoiler alert: You totally do!) Flip back through the robot profiles in this book to pick your favorite features and weapons. Think about the mechanics. How would your robot drive? How would it deploy its weapon? Think about how it looks. Do you have a favorite animal or fictional character? Could that inspire its appearance? Be creative! Anything is possible.

THE FUTURE OF BATTLEBOTS

You might have reached the end of this book, but this is just the beginning of an exciting new adventure. Now that you've discovered the secrets and tricks behind all the stars of BattleBots, you're armed with the most valuable and powerful thing a robotics builder needs: knowledge. You've got the inside edge. Now run with it and see where it takes you!

Check out the resources below to get started on your own journey in robotic combat. Keep in mind that your first bot won't be your last, and winning your first competition takes dedication and perseverance. Will you lead the next generation of robot builders?

And remember, the very first rule of bot building and battling is to stay safe! Make sure you are always supervised by an adult and are taking proper safety precautions. Protective gear is an absolute must! A good bot builder is a safe bot builder.

https://battlebots.com
https://www.fingertechrobotics.com
http://sparc.tools
https://www.robotcombatevents.com
https://www.idtech.com

See you in the BattleBox!